The Church
Rumor
Mill

Danny Shelton

Rp Remnant
Publications

Coldwater MI 49036
www.remnantpublications.com

Copyright © 2008
Remnant Publications
649 East Chicago Road
Coldwater MI 49036
517-279-1304
www.remnantpublications.com

All Rights Reserved
Printed in the USA

Copy editing by Debi Tesser
Cover design by Haley Trimmer
Text design by Greg Solie • AltamontGraphics.com

ISBN 978-1-933291-39-0

Table of Contents

Introduction

I once heard someone say, "No one seems happier doing evil than someone doing it in the name of God." Wow. As the expression goes, "That is deep."

Like all Christians, I consider myself to be a follower of God. Yet I have never "happily done evil" in His name—or have I?

No, I haven't killed millions of Christians like the papacy did during the Dark Ages, and I don't suppose you have either. I'm not a Jim Jones or David Koresh, and I've never encouraged people to take their own lives in the name of God.

Recently, I saw a video of a suicide bomber saying his final good-byes to family and friends. As he drove off to kill unsuspecting people as well as himself, he actually seemed quite "happy." The way he was smiling and waving, you'd have thought he was going to a church picnic. Yes, it does seem to be true that no one does evil more happily than a person believing that he—or she—is carrying out God's will.

Several years ago a man intended to kill me. He said the Lord had told him to do it. He didn't carry through on his threat, of course, or I wouldn't be writing this book today. I do believe, however, that without God's protection the event could have happened.

This man said he was a Christian. He had been in prison at least four times for various crimes. Though he had been guilty of robbery, as far as I know he had never committed murder. Yet, when he thought the Lord was speaking to him, he brought a large knife to my house.

He was ready to "carry out God's command," and if that meant killing me, so be it. Pretty scary, wouldn't you say?

Most Christians would agree that God wasn't behind the crimes of Jim Jones, David Koresh, or the papacy during the Dark Ages. These people weren't being used by God—they were pawns of the devil himself.

Whether for religious purposes or any other reason, physical killings in this day and age are not "politically correct." Most governments try to protect their citizens from terrible crimes by enforcing laws against violence, and rightfully so.

Professed Christians, however, are executing crimes today that don't get the slightest bit of attention from earthly governments. Such crimes do receive the attention of the heavenly government, for they have "killed" untold numbers of people. These crimes are spiritual killings.

I'm talking about the "church rumor mill," which seems to have made its way into just about every church in the world. Yes, this "mill" is alive and still churning out rumors in churches today. Somehow, Satan has deceived people into believing that the sins of gossip and slander won't keep them from heaven. This is another one of Satan's lies, of course.

Killing people physically is not the only way to destroy them. But we don't have to resort to physical killings. By destroying reputations and character, the church rumor mill effectively destroys people's lives. The results are disastrous: people who lose their reputations and credibility quite frequently lose even their will to live.

In this book, we will give credit where credit is due. We will give Satan the credit or blame for starting the first rumor mill while he was in heaven. We will also be called upon to do some real soul searching about our own Christian walk with God. Through reading this book, I hope each of us will prayerfully consider whether we are really walking with God or have, instead, fallen prey to one of Satan's greatest snares, the "church rumor mill."

The Bible's Anti-Rumor Mill Chapter

*T*hough I speak with the tongues of men and of angels, and have not charity, I am become as sounding brass, or a tinkling cymbal.

And though I have the gift of prophecy, and understand all mysteries, and all knowledge; and though I have all faith, so that I could remove mountains, and have not charity, I am nothing.

And though I bestow all my goods to feed the poor, and though I give my body to be burned, and have not charity, it profiteth me nothing.

Charity suffereth long, and is kind; charity envieth not; charity vaunteth not itself, is not puffed up, doth not behave itself unseemly, seeketh not her own, is not easily provoked, thinketh no evil; rejoiceth not in iniquity, but rejoiceth in the truth; beareth all things, believeth all things, hopeth all things, endureth all things.

Charity never faileth: but whether there be prophecies, they shall fail; whether there be tongues, they shall cease; whether there be knowledge, it shall vanish away. For we know in part, and we prophesy in part. But when that which is perfect is come, then that which is in part shall be done away.

When I was a child, I spake as a child, I understood as a child, I thought as a child: but when I became a man, I put away childish things. For now we see through a glass, darkly; but then face to face: now I know in part; but then shall I know even as also I am known.

And now abideth faith, hope, charity, these three; but the greatest of these is charity (1 Corinthians 13, KJV).

CHAPTER 1

The Booming "Business of Buzz"

Have you noticed that gossip is big business these days? We live in a culture where, in the minds of many people, information is gold. If you watch much entertainment TV, you know the "celebrity circuit" is the craze and craving of our time. In a virtual media frenzy, people want to know who's doing what, where they did it, how, with whom, and why. Whether it's Oprah's new diet, Britney's breakdown, or Tom Cruise's latest religion, the business of buzz is booming.

This should actually not be a surprise to Christians, since the Bible foretells that slander would be one of the signs of the end (2 Timothy 3:1). What is surprising, and even shocking at times, are the inroads that gossip has made *in the Christian church*.

Christians place a lot of emphasis on the Ten Commandments, and rightfully so. The injunctions to honor God, respect our parents, and refrain from killing or stealing (among others) are all important commandments to keep.

The ninth commandment, however, doesn't seem to get as much press as the rest. In fact this commandment, which warns us not to "bear false witness" against our neighbors, is likely the most frequently violated among Christian people. This is particularly alarming, since Christianity is really all about love, and true love is allergic to the very idea of slander.

The Bible tells us that "God is love" (1 John 4:8, 16). When Jesus lived on this earth, He demonstrated that love in quite a few ways. In fact, His life was the perfect example of love. When He left the courts above to live on this sinful earth, Jesus exemplified love. When He went about teaching, preaching, and healing, He showed us His love. When He separated Himself from the rules and regulations of religiosity, He taught that love was more than a set of stipulations. And when He went to the cross, loving us more than life or even Himself so that we who were born to die could live forever with Him, He showed us the ultimate love. Jesus didn't spend His time on earth for Himself. He lived a life filled with love, by helping others in every possible way. Because God is love, we can also be assured that God is fair and just. There are no walls of discrimination when it comes to God's love for His human creation.

Of course, the example of Jesus is quite a strong sermon for Christians. If we say we are Christians, we should be acting like Him. Our job is to uplift, encourage, and help those around us. God wants His church to actually be a sanctuary, or safe place, for those who are helpless and hurting. That sanctuary should reach out and help not only non-Christians around us, but Christians as well.

All too often, we Christians think it's our privilege to criticize and pass judgment on fellow believers. Rather than loving others as Jesus did, we add to their hurt. This spirit of criticism, of bearing false witness and wrongly judging each other, has always been one of the greatest enemies of the church. Church history is strewn with the victims of gossip and slander—and it's not a pretty sight. Unfortunately, this highly effective enemy is still prowling God's church today. When church members set themselves up as "judge, jury, and executioner" of fellow members, however, they are not following Christ, for that is not His way.

"Powering Down" God's Church

Satan knows very well that a purified, praying, and Spirit-filled church has power. He saw that power in action on the day of Pentecost, and rest assured that he never wants to see such a day again. That's why he's waging an all-out, no-holds-barred war against Christians who are eligible to receive the latter rain or outpouring of the Holy Spirit.

When Joel prophesied that "afterward I will pour out my Spirit upon all flesh ..." (Joel 2:28), he was really foretelling a final "nail in the coffin" for Satan. When the Latter Rain starts to fall, Satan knows what that means: the final end for himself and his followers, forever. That's why he wants so badly to "sift us as wheat," divide us, turn us inside out, and even against ourselves.

Satan knows, understands, and believes what the Bible says—that "a house divided against itself cannot stand ..." The last thing he wants is for modern-day Christians to come together in one accord—how much better for his cause to see us backbiting, bickering, and back-stabbing ourselves. Dreading the day when Christians shift their focus toward serving God and keeping his commandments, Satan is salvaging every trick to stop that day in its tracks. He knows very well what it means when, through prayer and study of God's Word, we put on the armor of God described in Ephesians 6, for when that armor is on, he can't deceive and destroy us.

A Very Successful Tactic

Throughout history, the evil one has been quite successful at persuading angels and humans to follow him. How did he accomplish this feat? He used gossip to influence those around him. Always the great deceiver, he won his first followers through artful, influential, and dishonest insinuations. Through the use of gossip, Satan was able to "adjust the attitudes" of God's holy angels from song, praise, and worship to criticism, faultfinding, and destruction. By evil-speaking and slander, he convinced approximately one-third of the holy angels to rebel against God forever. (Revelation 12:3, 4).

The very first "spin doctor" began his work right in heaven, by issuing "bad press releases" about God. No doubt he was a highly effective spammer, blogger, and seminar speaker as well—whatever it took to spread his message across the world.

So began Satan's fall from heaven, Lucifer's spiral from grace, and the very first rumor mill. The factory was erected, the machinery was put in place, and the mass production of gossip and slander began. I wish I could say this church rumor mill was short-lived, but unfortunately, its work of pulverization had only begun ...

CHAPTER 2

"Bad Press" in the Church of Heaven

I t's hard to understand how Lucifer, the most honored angel in the courts of heaven, somehow turned against God. By all outward appearances, he had everything going for him. The most important job heaven could offer, an "office" in the throne room of God, good looks, musical talent, and the adoration of other angels. His heavenly home, with its gem-studded walls, streets of gold, and singing angels, must have been a truly great place to live.

At one time, Lucifer undoubtedly had been incredibly happy. But somehow, the seeds of discontent began to enter his heart.

The Bible doesn't tell all the details of how sin grew in heaven. It's hard for our human minds to conceive how a created being like Lucifer could purpose in his heart to "unseat" the Creator of the universe. There was nothing but perfection around him, yet somehow, Lucifer chose to risk everything—even his eternal life—on an incredibly foolish gamble. I don't pretend to understand all of this, but I do understand that this fallen angel is to blame for sin in this world today.

Why did Satan rebel in the first place? We may not know all the reasons, but we do know that selfishness and greed were two of his motivations. When Satan said "I will be like the most High" (Isaiah 14:14), he coveted God's place as Creator. Satan's self-serving love for himself (which is still very much on display today) set him directly against God. It also separated him from God for eternity, for God is love, and selfishness goes against the very foundation of His government.

When Satan began to desire the position of God in heaven, he was actually breaking the tenth commandment: "Thou shalt not covet." When he succumbed to jealousy and began to exalt himself by criticizing God, he also broke the ninth commandment as well ("thou shalt not bear false witness").

Satan's sin, which began in his heart and mind, quickly progressed into physical action. While the sin began with a "simple" desire for self-promotion, it soon led to an all-out attempt to destroy another being (in this case, God Himself). Similarly, many people begin by breaking the ninth and/or tenth commandments (bearing false witness and/or coveting), and in the end, they break other commandments (stealing, killing, etc.) as well.

The Bible gives no evidence that the war in heaven was physical or fought with weapons. It never talks about "killing" in heaven, such as happens in earthly wars. Perhaps this is because no one, including Satan, can fight against God and win. Satan couldn't even have remained alive without God permitting it, for God is the source of life. The war between Christ and Satan, then, was a spiritual war, a war of words and ideas.

We know some of the ideas Satan set forth in this war because the Bible tells us that he said in his heart, "I will ascend into heaven, I will exalt my throne above the stars of God: I will sit also upon the mount of the congregation in the sides of the north: I will ascend above the heights of the clouds; I will be like the most High" (Isaiah 14:13, 14).

Satan was obviously intent on promoting himself. Untruths, slander, and gossip were some of the most effective tools in his arsenal, which is no doubt why Jesus referred to Satan as the "father of lies." God is all about truth and love, and the only way Satan could turn the angels against Him was to resort to rumors, truth-twisting, and falsehood.

Most gossipers like to be secretive, and Satan was no exception. He may have worked in the throne room of God, but you can be sure he went elsewhere to whisper his accusations. Why all this secrecy? Because when things are secret, the talebearer has much more freedom to add to, subtract from, or twist the story without being held responsible for damage done to the victim of the rumor. Furthermore, the tale changes as each individual tells his or her own version.

Satan started his political campaign against God quietly. He became bolder, however, as the heat of battle increased. Soon he was making public statements, and probably even issued a few "bad press releases" about God.

Satan had several advantages in this war of words. Since he didn't abide by the rules of love, he didn't have to play fair. He could—and did—twist God's words without restraint. Evil knows no boundaries, and Satan wasn't about to let any requirements to "tell the truth" impede his diabolical mission to steal, kill, and destroy.

In the heavenly court of public opinion, our loving God wasn't exactly playing on a level playing field. While He wanted to convince the angels that what He was doing was right, He also chose to fight this spiritual war as a God of truth and love. That means God would not lie, slander, gossip, or twist the truth.

Satan, on the other hand, was playing by no such rules. The angels revered and loved Satan because he had been their leader. Also, no one had ever previously lied to them. Satan had been very close to God, so they figured he must know what he was talking about. They also simply expected that he would tell the truth. Because Satan doesn't play by the same law of eternal love that God does, he had a real advantage in the heavenly battle, just as he does now on earth. The good news in this scenario is that Satan's advantage will only last for a short period of time, as Jesus has promised to come back to this earth a second time. The second time He will come as King of Kings to save His people from the grasp of Satan for all eternity.

The devil made the most of his advantage in his efforts to sway many of God's angels to his side in the battle for supremacy in heaven. Bible scholars commonly believe that one third of the angels of heaven left the service of God to follow Satan, and that these angels were "cast" to the earth, along with their leader, by God. This belief was based on Revelation 12, where John the Revelator states that "there was war in heaven: Michael and his angels fought against the dragon: and the dragon fought and his angels and prevailed not; neither was their place found any more in heaven. And the great dragon was cast out, that old serpent, called the DEVIL, and Satan, which deceiveth the whole world: he was cast out into the earth, and his angels were cast out with him." Revelation 12:4 also says, "And his tail (the dragon's) drew the third part of the stars of heaven, and did cast them to the earth ..."

Although we don't know exactly how many angels fell along with Satan, we do know that Satan has a great many demons in his army. These demons, which were once heavenly angels, now stand ready to do Satan's bidding.

No doubt some of the angels challenged God to defend Himself against Satan's attacks. Others may have encouraged Him to destroy Satan in order to stop the insurrection that was beginning to take place in heaven.

As momentum grew for Satan's rebellion, he became bolder and bolder against God. Having convinced himself that he was right in his accusations, he began to attack the very character of God.

God doesn't force His laws upon His creatures, so His defense against Satan was to allow sin to run its course. Satan's rebellion must play out. Then the heavenly host could see that sin against the creator God would ultimately lead to death. Many untrue and unfair rumors had been spread, but He did not become angry and destroy the sinning angels. Because there is no life apart from the Creator, God knew that those who chose to remain in sin would destroy themselves soon enough.

Actually, Satan doesn't care how humans are destroyed. Whether he destroys us, or we destroy each other, is of no real concern to him. Over the centuries he has adapted his tactics. Sometimes he has resorted to spiritual violence, and sometimes to physical destruction. Through it all, however, one factor has remained diabolically constant: the "rumor mill" continues to grind.

CHAPTER 3

Treacherous, Traitorous Times

For most of earth's history, Satan has used fear, intimidation, and physical harm as his *modus operandi*. This was particularly evident during the era of the Dark Ages. Without God as the head, history records that religion and man-made governments can be very dangerous to society. Jesus and virtually all His disciples lost their lives at the hands of a misguided religious people and government.

It's also a matter of recorded history that most wars are fought over religion. Even today, the wars in the Middle East are a continuation of wars that have been waging for thousands of years, mostly over religious differences. The Bible foretold that there would be continual conflict: "And you will hear of wars and rumors of wars. See that you are not troubled; for all these things must come to pass, but the end is not yet, for nation will rise against nation, and kingdom against kingdom" (Matthew 24:6, 7).

In the time of Christ, the Jewish leaders took their eyes off the Savior and appointed themselves as judge, jury, and executioner of all who opposed them. In essence, they appointed themselves as "God on earth."

During the Middle Ages, the great religious powers also fell into Satan's trap. Their desire for world dominance and the allegiance of their subjects reigned supreme. Like the Jews before them, they tried to play God, appointing themselves to judge all who disagreed.

The Church of Rome was not built on Jesus' admonition to "love thy neighbour as thyself" (Matthew 19:19). As it gathered great power and influence, it seemed bent on taking the life of anyone who opposed its man-made laws of religion. The resulting conflict seemed to be only a continuation of the war fought in heaven, the working out of Jesus' words in John 10:10 saying that "the thief (Satan) comes but for to kill, steal and to destroy." Papal Rome had taken on the Spirit of Satan wrapped in the garb of Christianity.

History records that Satan used this "church" to kill millions of people. During the Dark Ages alone, an estimated 50 to 75 million people lost their lives at the hands of the Church of Rome.

Of course it was an effort on Satan's part to stop Christianity from spreading to the whole world. His plan backfired. As more and more persecution was perpetrated by papal Rome, Christians began to flee to new areas of the world carrying their hand-copied Scriptures and bringing God into their hearts. They shared with everyone they could about the love of God and righteousness by faith. Thus, the gospel began to spread rapidly to the whole world.

Untold multitudes of people were burned at the stake during the Dark Ages because they wouldn't renounce their belief in God and succumb to the authority of the Roman church, and they died in the Lord. Satan was defeated, and those children of God who gave their lives for Christ now await the second coming to gain victory over death, hell and the grave.

"How did Satan react to this defeat?" "Has he given up his fight to steal, kill, and destroy as described in John 10:10? Or has he just changed his tactics of destruction?"

The answer is that Satan is doing just what he has always done. He has moved away from using the church to physically kill millions of people as this is no longer "politically correct." Instead, he is killing them spiritually. Finding that the blood of martyrs was like seed, Satan switched his focus to spreading lies about the creator God through the governments of the world, the institutions of higher learning, and yes, even the Christian churches.

As the nations became more civilized and sophisticated, Satan began to use other means to take control of his subjects. Having been unsuccessful in his attempts to kill all Christians, he began to attack Christianity using tactics such as the perversion of science. With the encouragement of Satan, men began to think they were more intelligent than God, which was the same strategy Satan had used in heaven to deceive the angels.

Evolution, which is really a direct attack against God and the Christian faith, was orchestrated by none other than Satan himself.

"I shall be like the most High," Satan had said in heaven, so he influenced scientists to write books attacking the creation story told in the Bible. When learned men rejected the truth and began to teach others the same, Satan rejoiced. His dream of becoming "like the most High" to the people of planet Earth was finally coming true. Human beings worshiped him in spite of themselves. Evolution was his lie. When humans accepted Darwin's theory of evolution, they were indeed endorsing Satan; therefore, they chose him over the creator God.

"How could this be?" When men reject God as their creator, they accept Satan's lie that there is no God. Darwin didn't come up with the theory of evolution—Satan did. Yes, he has used Darwin and thousands of others like him over the years, but they were only pawns in his hands.

The acceptance of evolution was quite a change in belief for people in the United States. Young America was a nation built on Christian principles. After Christopher Columbus first came to America in 1492, this nation grew rapidly. People left Europe in droves, looking for a better life and attempting to escape religious persecution. Our country's forefathers had the courage to lay plans for a government that believed in separation of church and state, and even penned a Constitution that boldly acknowledged there was a creator God who sustained life. How else could you explain the phrase in the Constitution, declaring that "all men are *created* equal?"

Things began to change when America built its own government-controlled educational system. These great institutions of higher learning began to adopt Darwin's theory of evolution, denying an all powerful creator God as the reason for human existence. They began to teach that mankind was not created by God as stated in the Bible, but that the human race had evolved over millions and millions of years, progressing from the tiniest cell into the complicated human beings that we are today. The "survival of the fittest" attitude, a selfish concept which has opened the door to much trouble in our world today, springs from this lack of belief in a creator God.

"I will take what is mine because I am the fittest" is the mantra of many. "I will take whatever I want."

Today the damaging theory of evolution is taught not only in the colleges and universities of America, but in many other countries. It is also taught in the public high schools, and even at the elementary school level. Satan's lie about God is promoted around the world.

This confusion about who God is, whether there is a God, and truth in general, is Satan's greatest accomplishment. The Bible says that if we know the truth, the truth will set us free (John 8:32). We do not have to fall for Satan's lies, nor do we have to be separated from God for eternity.

"I am the way, the *truth* and the life," Jesus says (John 14:6, emphasis supplied). Satan is only afraid of one thing, and that is Jesus Christ because He is truth. The devil attacks that truth by continuing to spread his lies about God. He is also happy to spread lies about God's people. Having temporarily laid aside his all-out effort to kill all Christians physically, he has resorted to a different, but equally deadly, tactic of "spiritual killings."

Gossip, slander, and backbiting are all "arrows" in the quiver he uses to perpetrate these killings, and he is especially pleased when professed Christians actually aid him in this work. Christians of today like to think they are more civilized than God's people of the past.

"We would never have murmured against Moses," they say. "We certainly would have recognized Christ as the Messiah. And as for the persecutions during the Dark Ages, they were truly despicable. We would never hurt other followers of God in that manner."

While these claims sound quite convincing on the surface, upon closer examination there really is a heart-wrenching question we all need to ask ourselves: are we really any better when it comes to treating others with love and Christian consideration, than our more "barbaric" brethren of the past?

CHAPTER 4

Are We Really Better?

Most modern-day Christians like to think that the church today is "kinder and gentler" than the medieval church that persecuted fellow Christians by torture and killing. Looking back at history, it doesn't take a rocket scientist to figure out that Satan was in charge of that murderous movement.

When we compare the medieval Church of Rome to the Christian church of today, it does seem that today's church passes the grade with flying colors. Compared to times past, many parts of the world enjoy remarkable levels of religious freedom. Most governments allow Bibles to be printed in their respective languages by the millions every year. Nearly all major bookstores around the world contain numerous books about Christianity, church growth, and numerous other subjects pertaining to the Christian faith. Many major church denominations also support missionaries stationed around the world for the express purpose of converting the non-Christians to Christianity.

Upon closer examination, we have to wonder if the atmosphere in churches today is really much better than during the Dark Ages. It is true; our society does not allow the physical murder of one human being by another without punishment to the perpetrator. Even the godless governments of the world recognize that civilizations can't exist without laws to protect their people.

As Christians, we are usually quick to judge and condemn others who commit physical acts of violence. We know that murder is a violation of God's law, which equates to sin. What many Christians fail to realize is that to sin against others in our hearts is just as bad as physical sin. Whether overt or concealed, sin can keep us separated from God for eternity. As a friend of mine often says, "The devil doesn't care over which side of the boat we fall, just as long as we fall out."

While Satan still inspires physical persecution wherever the opportunity arises, he has been especially successful with his strategy of encouraging "spiritual killings" within God's church. Satan loves to use people—even professed Christians—to destroy the reputations of the followers of Jesus by attacking their characters. The same devil who released bad press reports about God in heaven is now providing "free" bad press to those who have given their lives to Jesus. Unfortunately for all involved, the "church rumor mill" which worked so effectively to deceive a third of the angels of heaven, seems to be quite alive and well today.

The only big difference between Satan's strategy from so many years ago, and his strategy now, is that he has so many more helpers. Satan loves to use the unconverted hearts of human beings to fulfill his devious plans of destruction for the whole human race.

Because of the confusion and doubt that Satan has put into men's minds, "spiritual killings" are now at an all-time high. When people of the earth reject God, they automatically reject the great commandment of Jesus to "love thy neighbor as thyself." They cannot love their neighbor as themselves, no matter how hard they try. Only as people accept Jesus and take on His nature can they love their neighbor as themselves.

I once heard the tragic story of two elderly women pianists, both of whom attended the same small church. Each of these two dear ladies wanted to be the "official" pianist for the church, which put the pastor and congregation in the somewhat uncomfortable position of designating who would hold the position each year. The church solved the problem by voting the ladies "in" on alternating years, so that each had a turn to be the official pianist while the other would be the assistant.

This seemed like a good solution to the church members and their pastor, who did their best to keep both pianists happy. Their best efforts were in vain; one Sunday morning, just after the annual "official pianist election," the weekly church service took a terrible turn. The newly elected official pianist had just taken her position to play for the morning worship service when the other woman walked into the church. Without hesitation, she went right up to the front, pulled a gun from her purse, and shot the other pianist to death.

"How could this happen in a Christian church?" Did the elderly "gunwoman" not realize that killing another human being was a sin against God and His commandments? Was she ignorant of God's law? Or had she lost sight of the principles of true Christianity (that we should love one another)?

Did you notice any similarity between the lady pianist and the story of Lucifer's fall, as told in chapter two? Like Lucifer, this poor elderly lady was breaking the tenth commandment by coveting the position of another. Like Lucifer, she also quite likely broke the ninth commandment by gossiping about her fellow pianist. By dwelling on her covetous words and thoughts, she eventually talked herself into breaking another commandment, "Thou shalt not kill," by pulling the trigger.

How could a woman who had served her church so many years come to the place where she could calmly walk into her church and commit a terrible murder in violation of the very principles of Christianity she claimed to uphold? It seems safe to say that the killing resulted from an earlier sin in this woman's life—a sin which may very well have gone unnoticed by others—the sin of covetousness.

What else but uncontrolled covetousness could "trigger" an elderly lady to terminate her fellow pianist, at the front of the church, no less? The woman who pulled the gun most likely knew much about God's laws. But even though she knew it was wrong to kill, it was the great principle undergirding Christianity that she could no longer see. True Christianity, as described by Jesus, says we should love one another (John 13:34, 35).

The gunwoman was also more concerned about pleasing her physical, earthly, or fleshly desires than she was about pleasing Jesus, following His Word, and loving her fellow man. Hard feelings arose in her heart, and her physical nature won over her spiritual nature.

As shocking and bizarre as this story seems, similar episodes are being "repeated" in churches around the world today as we "slay" one another with verbiage. Often times so-called Christians gather information against a head elder or a pastor.

"Surely this information is true," they tell each other because it came from a reliable source. In such cases, we should use the Bible route (Matthew 18:15-17) to deal with such problems. Too often we make judgments on hearsay alone. Sadly, I've also seen cases where a pastor becomes part of the rumor mill problem rather than using the Word of God to counsel folk to find the truth of a given situation.

I believe in accountability within the church, especially when it comes to leadership. However, I also believe that we must not fall into the temptation of judging others without a real knowledge of the truth. We are not the judge of our fellowman. God is. This is because we can't know what another human being is really thinking, what is in his or her heart, or what the circumstances truly are. In the words of the Bible, "Man looketh upon the outward appearance, but the Lord looketh on the heart" (1 Samuel 16:7).

I've been in full-time ministry for nearly 25 years, and nearly all the biggest spiritual battles I have fought have been with professed Christians. Am I down on Christians? Of course not! I too profess to be a Christian, and over the years I too have been guilty of doing harm against the cause of God without even realizing it. Satan targets everyone. He is no respecter of persons.

One pastor gathered negative information about a ministry from the Internet, and then he forwarded it to his members at church.

"Why would you bring this to church?" some of his members wanted to know. "Have you checked with the ministry involved to see if these things are true? Why would you bring us these slanderous accusations, without even checking on them?"

"I want you to know the 'truth,'" the pastor replied. Somehow, by dredging up and spreading unsubstantiated claims against a Christian ministry, he thought he was doing God service. What was really happening, of course, was that Satan was distracting both the pastor and the congregation from what they should really be doing. How well he knows that when we focus on the faults of others, it's impossible to be in an attitude of praise and worship to our heavenly Father.

Do you think this pastor—or any honest Christian for that matter—honestly believes he (or she) can stand justified before God when they spread gossip about Christian ministries that they don't even know are true? True Christians know that Jesus doesn't condone the spreading of gossip, accusations against other Christians, or anything else for that matter. Nowhere does the Bible sanction acts of gossip or defamation of character through Word of mouth, the printed page, Internet, radio, TV, or any other mode of communication.

Gossipers Like to "Keep Secrets"

Most people don't want to be seen or quoted as a gossip, so they like to whisper their accusations in secret. They use phrases like: "Have you heard … ?" "They say that …" Sneaking around, by the way, is one clear sign that something is of the devil. Our God is a God of truth. He and His workers do not have to "sneak" around.

This desire to be secretive is probably one of the reasons why so many who call themselves Christians use chat rooms to interact on the Internet. Not all chat room communications are bad, of course. It is truly shocking to realize how many people are using Christian chat rooms to literally destroy the reputations of others.

Most of these communications are made under false names, so the perpetrators of the gossip can't be identified. Amazingly, these chat room "pros" don't realize that our Lord and Savior Jesus Christ knows their identity. They can't hide who they are from Him. Even more amazing is the fact that so many professed Christians log in to these chat rooms to read the slander and accusations against their fellow Christians. They may even "forward" the rumor mill to others or continue to spread the gossip by word of mouth.

Why all this secrecy? Because when things are secret, people have much more freedom to add to, subtract from, or twist the story without being responsible for the damage done to the victim of the rumor.

An explanation of the difference between gossip and slander has been floating around the Internet. According to the definition, gossiping is like coming up close to a person with a loaded machine gun and blowing them off the face of the earth. In contrast, slander involves buying a higher-powered rifle with a scope, and, by sneaking and sniping, finishing off the person in such a way that they never knew what hit them.

Did you notice anything here? One method is more open, and one is more secretive. With both methods, however, the end result is the same. Like the elderly pianist in the church, the person being targeted—or at least their reputation—is dead.

When I was an employer, one of the hardest things for me to do was let an employee go. Whether I had to fire them or simply ask them to leave, it never was easy.

In one situation I remember, I had tried every possible means of reconciling the employee in question with other workers around him, including myself. After much prayer, I finally decided to ask him to leave his employment. With the board of director's approval, the ministry I worked for even gave him several thousand dollars in severance pay. Our hope was that this money would reassure him that neither I nor the administrative team were his enemies. But while we cared about him and his family, the best situation for everyone involved was to separate our employer-employee relationship.

Instead of being grateful that we didn't fire him and leave a bad mark on his employment record, this now ex-employee began to circulate bad information about myself and other members of the administration. Story after story began to surface about how unfairly he had been treated. This went on for months as he visited both church members and employees in an effort to gather support for himself.

This ex-employee and myself both had a mutual friend whom we both respected and who was an attorney. In an effort to bring some closure to the whole thing, I asked our attorney friend if he would talk to the former employee and hear his story. After hearing both "sides" of the story, I asked the attorney to bring me an honest evaluation of the whole situation.

The attorney went to the home of the ex-employee, and they talked for nearly four hours. After their meeting, the attorney returned to me with his evaluation as promised.

"I know this man professes to be a Christian," the attorney said, "but I see no hope for forgiveness or reconciliation on his part at this time."

"Some time ago I was involved as an attorney in a murder trial," my friend continued. "For hours we listened to the accused murderer explain why he had shot and killed the victim. While this man admitted killing his victim, he also tried to justify the murder. He had so much hatred in his heart for the victim, he deceived himself into thinking he did the right thing."

I'll never forget what my attorney friend said to me next.

"The only difference between your ex-employee and the murderer is that the murderer actually pulled the trigger of a gun and killed his victim. Your ex-employee has killed you too—in his heart and mind."

The former employee's justification for "destroying" my character was the same type of reasoning espoused by the convicted murderer.

"I pointed him to Scripture that showed what he was doing was unchristian and sinful," the attorney explained, "but the man kept on defending himself."

"I know what you are saying, BUT ..." he would tell the attorney. Then he continued to give his reasons why the character assassination attack he was implementing was not really sin even though it was contrary to biblical teaching. This person was so wrapped in his hatred that he couldn't see that his actions were contrary to that of a Christian.

"He is just as deceived by Satan as the murderer in that trial, who is now serving a long-term sentence in the federal prison," the attorney commented. "The only difference was that the ex-employee had committed a killing in his heart, while the murderer had committed a physical murder. Both were sins against God's law of "Thou shalt not kill."

Unfortunately, this same type of "spiritual killing" happens quite frequently in Christian churches today. Spiritual warfare because of jealousy takes root between church members, and "character assassinations" are planned and/or executed.

This is nothing new, of course, for Satan has been using the very same tactic for thousands of years. He has not changed his mode of operation, not in the least. As the Bible tells us in Revelation 12:9, 10, he is the "accuser of the brethren." He loves to plant seeds of jealousy, covetousness, and pride in the unconverted heart. After "the planting," he waters those seeds and watches them grow into spiritual and sometimes physical action against other people, and ultimately, against God.

It doesn't have to be this way, of course. We Christians do not have to give in to the devil's temptations. The battle begins in the heart.

CHAPTER 5

Straight Talk to Pastors

I realize this chapter may not be the most popular among Christian readers, but I write it because I believe that it bears hearing. It seems too many preachers today spend a great deal of their time preaching on subjects that do not "ruffle the feathers" of the hearers by telling them the truth. Satan has many detours to place before Christians to lead them away from heaven. The Christian walk is not always easy. In fact, the Bible says that all who live godly lives *shall* suffer persecution. The Bible also says, "Be ye doers of the word, and not hearers only ..." (James 1:22). In other words, there is more to living a Christian life than just getting saved.

For several reasons, far too many preachers seem content in just talking about the love of God. Don't get me wrong; nothing is more important in the whole universe than the fact that God loves each and every one of us. But God's love for us alone will not save us: "For God so loved the world, that He gave His only begotten Son, that whosoever believeth in Him should not perish, but have everlasting life" (John 3:16). We have to believe in the saving power of Jesus Christ in order to be saved. If we deny the power of Christ and do not accept His free gift of grace, according to the Bible we cannot be saved.

Acts 4:12 says, "Neither is there salvation in any other: for there is none other name under heaven given among men, whereby we must be saved." Praise God. We are indeed saved by grace. But for the pastor and fellow Christian we need to understand that our spiritual battle has just begun.

We just read where Christians are to be doers of the Word. When we dedicate our lives to the service of God, Satan becomes even more furious with us and his attacks will worsen. While we can read a Bible on our own, I believe that we each need a church family and a pastor dedicated to unmasking Satan and his detours for us, whatever the cost. I realize that this is not always easy, but I'm sure the road to Calvary was not always easy for the Master teacher as He traveled this path.

While pastors preach what people want to hear rather than what they need to hear for a variety of reasons, I will allude to only a couple of the more obvious reasons: job security and church growth. Actually, the two are very much related. Church growth usually means job security for most pastors. Truth has never really been popular among many Christian people because when one learns truth, it usually means changing one's habits or lifestyle. Let's face it; change is quite difficult for most people.

They seem to have forgotten the admonition found in 2 Timothy 4:3-5: "For the time will come when they will not endure sound doctrine: but after their own lusts shall they heap to themselves teachers having itching ears; and they shall turn away their ears from the truth, and shall be turned unto fables. But watch thou in all things, endure afflictions, do the work of an evangelist, full proof of thy ministry."

I believe the devil works hard to ensure that God's people become comfortable in their chosen lifestyles. The devil is content with us when we are in "a rut." Simply put, the Revelation term Laodicea means complacency or, even better, "spiritually asleep." As already discussed, Revelation 3 explains that God's last-day generation of people are seen by Him as wretched, miserable, poor, blind, and naked. Revelation also tells us that the Laodicean church sees themselves as rich and increased with goods and has need of nothing. If this is the case, and I believe with all my heart that it is, then preachers should be preaching as they've never before preached about the power of God and urgency in their lives to lead people to see themselves for what they really are. We are all sinners in need of a Savior.

The road to heaven means more than just saying "I do." Just like wedding vows, "I do" is just the beginning, not the whole marriage or the end. Too many ministers seem to teach that when people accept Jesus as Lord and Savior of their lives, the mission is accomplished, which, of course, is not true. It is only the beginning. Salvation calls for reformation in the life of an individual.

Once a couple unites in holy matrimony, they may take years before they really unite as one. Why? Because during all of our years of singlehood, we are focused on doing what's best for "me." That is not all bad, of course. Decisions must be made. What goals am I going to strive to accomplish in my life? What will be my education level? What will ultimately be my occupation? Where will I reside? What about retirement?

Also, when two people unite in marriage, they share in a transformation and uniting that takes place and continues "until death due us part." It's the same thing when one accepts Jesus as Lord and Savior of their life. They are no longer living for self. A transformation takes place and continues the rest of our lives as long as we partner or become one with Christ. Marriage and Christianity both mean transformation and work in order to be successful.

As a new Christian, we might ask ourselves very similar questions. What goals am I striving to accomplish in my Christian walk with Christ? How much time am I willing to devote to spreading the gospel of Christ? Where will my residence for eternity be?

While getting "saved" is the greatest event in the human life on this earth, it is only the beginning. But many preachers seem hesitant to preach transformation and change because they are not popular subjects. Moreover, if we do change, we usually like changes to come slowly in our lives. But I want to take time to encourage pastors to give the trumpet a certain sound. Remember what Paul wrote, "And even things without life giving sound, whether pipe or harp, except they give a distinction in the sounds, how shall it be known what is piped or harped? For if the trumpet give an uncertain sound, who shall prepare himself to the battle?" (1 Corinthians 14:7, 8).

When we read the Bible, we can quickly see that there is and has been a great controversy between good and evil raging for thousands of years. Since planet Earth, as we know it, will soon end, now is the time to give the trumpet a certain sound!

Instead of calling ministers to be concerned about winning popularity contests, God calls men and women in His service to proclaim the truth of Jesus who was sent to save a lost-and-dying world.

Even though we still have a few preachers who will proclaim the undiluted truth of the gospel, many listeners either have selective hearing and want to hear only those things they can easily incorporate into their lives, or they are very quick to digest what they hear and then direct it to someone else. It is much easier, after all, to digest instruction from God's Word when we apply it to someone else's life. I think if we are honest, most of us will agree that we have been guilty of applying a good sermon from our pastor to another person who we feel needs the instruction worse than we do.

One of the Christian church's biggest fears should be that of compromise. God says in Revelation that He sees our works, and He would rather that we be either "hot or cold" rather than be lukewarm, or He will reject us. It seems to me that being lukewarm is a compromise or dilution of the mission of the Christian church as designated by God.

Speaking from a common sense point of view, hot or cold water makes a distinct impact when it comes in contact with the bare human skin. When water is lukewarm it is barely even noticed. One would doubtful fall asleep in a tub of scalding hot water or a tub of ice water. But on the other hand it seems only too easy to fall asleep in a tub full of lukewarm water. It seems that Revelation 3 is a call to the entire body of Christ to wake up from Laodicea and repent before it is forever too late.

While salvation is an individual choice, I believe that those in leadership will be held responsible when we stand before God if they have failed to give the trumpet the certain sound. Many pastors still teach the importance of keeping God's Ten Commandments in our hearts. They will preach that people should honor their father and mother, we shouldn't use the Lords' name in vain, and that we shouldn't place any other gods before the creator God. Some pastors will instruct people in the keeping of God's Holy Sabbath, condemn stealing, etc.

But sadly, many seem hesitant to talk about some of the other commandments. One of those, of course, is, "Thou shalt not kill." Too many pastors choose to ignore this commandment because it is far more challenging when they dig below the surface and not always politically correct.

I recently had one pastor tell me that since God gives us freedom to choose, that he felt that women should also have the choice to choose life or death for their baby. Isn't it amazing that a pastor would believe that it would not be breaking the sixth commandment when it comes to killing an unborn baby but upholds the commandment when it comes to killing his neighbor? I'm a firm believer that immoral issues such as abortion should not be put to a vote because our creator God has already settled the issue in His sixth commandment to us.

Even less popular among many ministers and their parishioners of the gospel today is commandment number nine, "Thou shalt not bear false witness against thy neighbor." This is one commandment that has become a less popular sermon topic over the years because its abuse has become more prevalent and acceptable.

Pastors know very well that when they try to shut down the church rumor mill through their preaching against backbiting, gossip, slander, lies, innuendos, etc., that people begin to get edgy and uncomfortable. Since most of us are guilty at one time or another of joining the church rumor mill, we often are offended and believe that the pastor is pointing a finger at us individually. Typically, when people regularly feel uncomfortable sitting through their pastor's sermon week after week, the church rumor mill begins to churn with a frenzy. The gears are overheated with blame laid on the pastor for "harping," or being out of balance, in his sermons, putting too much emphasis on "works." Next, the backbiters begin to accuse him of being a legalist trying to coax people to work their way into heaven. A church board meeting follows an elders' meeting, so the rotation of the rumor mill never stops. This is why we have pastors who preach only what the people want to hear.

Again, I praise God for pastors that are willing to stand firmly for truth and feed the congregation what they need to hear from the Word of God rather than dilute their messages to soften the sound to the ear.

CHAPTER 6

The Battle Between Two Natures

When people say bad things about me, I tend to want to defend myself. This is human nature, and it is also exactly what's wrong with defending one's self. When we try to fight our own battles and defend our own selves, it is our human nature—rather than God's spiritual nature—working in us.

At one point, people were writing things about me that were untrue. They were distributing terrible things about my character and attacking my family as well.

"If this story they're telling gets out, people might believe it," I thought. So I decided to defend myself. My strategy was either to go on my TV program and expose the ones who were telling the lies, or write a rebuttal and distribute it widely. Very quickly, however, the Lord prompted me not to do either of these things. I wasn't happy with that, so I argued with God.

"I have to defend myself against these lies," I told God. "If I don't, people might believe them, and not support my ministry anymore." I also reminded God that I wasn't guilty of these accusations, so I felt that I needed to offer a rebuttal.

When I quit talking and was willing to listen, the Lord told me that I needed to let Him defend me because I was guilty.

"But Lord, I'm not guilty of what these people are saying about me," I argued again.

"As a born sinner, you cannot defend yourself," was the Lord's reply. "Even though you are not guilty of what those people are writing, you need to trust God to be your defense attorney. God also reminded me that I needed to get to the point in my relationship with Him that I trusted Him with my life, all of the time.

That's the way it is with all of us, really. We have to let Jesus be our full-time attorney, or we will lose Him by trusting our lives into our own hands. This is when the "rubber really meets the road," when our faith in God and trust in His Word are really put to the test. When the going gets rough, and others are on the attack, who will we trust? Will we trust Jesus? Or do we trust only ourselves?

Each of us has two natures that are constantly battling for control—the physical and the spiritual. It would be nice if pastors and long-time Christians were exempt from this spiritual warfare, but such is not the case. The battle continues to rage for every one of our souls.

While the spiritual nature draws us to be like our loving Jesus, our physical nature leads us away from Jesus. This "earthly" side is all about pleasing "me, myself, and I." This great controversy between Christ and Satan has been going on for thousands of years, with the ultimate question to be answered for every one of us being this: Who will control our eternal destiny? Will we accept Gods free gift of salvation and spend eternity in heaven with Jesus? Or will we be separated from our loving God for eternity?

Because of the sin of Adam and Eve, mankind has taken on a sinful nature. This sinful nature is actually Satan's character in human form. We are born selfish. If you don't believe me just watch any small child. They naturally don't want to share what they have with others. They seem to only care about themselves. They love attention almost from the time they are born, and they easily get angry when things don't go their way. In essence, a small child seems to believe that the whole world revolves around them. Yes, we are born with a sinful nature, but praise God, Jesus came to free us from the prison of sin that Satan devised to ensnare us with.

Now, don't take me wrong. I did not say that we become perfect when we surrender our lives to Jesus. We should indeed become more and more Christlike with each passing day that we live here on earth. This is called the process of sanctification: growing closer to Christ by forsaking this world's sinful nature as we draw closer to Jesus. It is the working of a lifetime. All Christians fall short of the mark of being a follower of Jesus from time to time. But when we are sorry that we failed to represent Jesus rightly, and confess this to Him, He will once again forgive us from our sins and cleanse us from all unrighteousness (1 John 1:9). I call this living in the spirit vs. living in the flesh.

"If it feels good … DO IT!" The mantra of the hippy culture during the 1960s and 70s was all about feeding the earthly nature. But if we feed something, it will grow. If our focal point on earth is pleasing our physical senses of touch, taste, sight, hearing, and smell, we are pleasing our fleshly or beastly nature. If we allow that nature to grow unchecked, it will lead us to destruction not only in this earthly life, but for eternity. Every moment of every day, we are choosing which one of our natures to feed, and we can be sure of this: whichever nature we feed most on a daily basis will be the one that is strongest.

Thankfully, we do not have to succumb to our carnal natures. The Bible tells us that, while we were born with a carnal, self-serving nature, we can offset and even overcome it when we concentrate on spiritual values. As Christians, we should all be following the admonition of Paul to "put ye on the Lord Jesus Christ, and make not provision for the flesh, to fulfill the lusts thereof" (Romans 13:14).

Then our sinful, or carnal nature of Satan, will be nailed to the cross forever, and we will be able to take on the character of Jesus for eternity. Paul tells us at the last trump, when the dead in Christ shall rise first from the grave, we will shed our human or mortal nature. The Bible puts it this way:

And as we have borne the image of the earthy, we shall also bear the image of the heavenly. Now this I say brethren, that flesh and blood cannot inherit the kingdom of God: Neither doth corruption inherit incorruption. Behold, I show you a mystery: We shall not all sleep, but we shall all be changed, In a moment, in a twinkling of an eye, at the last trump: for the trumpet shall sound and the dead shall be raised incorruptible, and we shall be changed. For this corruption must put on incorruption and this mortal shall put on immortality. So when this corruption shall put on incorruption and this mortal shall put on immortality, then shall be brought to pass the saying that is written, Death is swallowed up in VICTORY. O death where is thy sting? O grave where is thy Victory? The sting of death is sin: and the strength of sin is the law, But thanks be to God, which giveth us the Victory through our Lord Jesus Christ. Therefore my beloved brethren, be ye steadfast, unmovable, always abounding in the work of the Lord, inasmuch, as ye know that your labor in not in vain in the Lord. (1 Corinthians 15: 49-58)

Amen! Praise the Lord! God's Word assures us of eternal salvation with Jesus if we simply confess that we are sinners and then go and tell what Jesus has done for us. Our Lord will take our sinful nature and in exchange give us His perfect nature. God understands we are dealing with our human tendency to fall into sin.

It's important for us to realize that since we are sinners, we can do nothing to save ourselves: "For all have sinned, and come short of the glory of God" (Romans 3:23). We must confess our sins to Jesus, for "if we confess our sins, He is faithful and just to forgive us our sins, and to cleanse us from all unrighteousness" (1 John 1:9).

Then what do we do? We must tell the world what Jesus has done for us. We must tell them that we have died to sin, in the spiritual sense, and because Jesus shed His blood on the cross of Calvary for an atonement for our sins that we can now have eternal life in heaven for ever with Jesus.

CHAPTER 7

The Problem at the Heart of the Matter

When I was young, many Christians wouldn't allow a TV in their homes. But then along came "family friendly" programs like *I Love Lucy, Leave it to Beaver, My Three Sons,* and a myriad of other options that seemed entertaining to the whole family. Many Christians, who were lulled to sleep by this apparently innocent snare, didn't seem to notice as more and more programs involving drugs, violence, and sex came right into their homes. Once we let our guard down, Satan loses no time taking up residence in our hearts.

I once heard of a Christian family that had the reputation for having the highest moral and religious standards. Then one day, as the story goes, they let a "stranger" into the house to live with them. The stranger had many fascinating stories to tell that the whole family would spend hours and hours listening to them. Though the parents in the home neither smoked nor drank, they let this stranger bring both of these bad habits right into their home. It didn't seem to bother dad, either, when the stranger would use bad language that had never before been allowed in his home.

As you may have guessed by now, the stranger was a television set. Many professed Christians spend hours each week watching TV programs that do not bring glory to God. Magazines, music, and the Internet also frequently bring bad habits into homes that would normally not have been allowed.

When I was a child, my mother used to sing a song that went something like this: "If Jesus came to your house to spend a day or two, if he came unexpected, I wonder what you'd do." The song goes on to ask if you would continue listening to your radio programs and using the same language you normally do. It also asks if we would find it hard to say grace at the table if Jesus were in our midst, or if we would have to change our conversation if He were to come for a visit. Near the end of the song the question is asked "Would you want Jesus to live with you forever or would you be glad when he left?"

What about our homes today? There are many worldly influences infiltrating our homes. Radio, TV, and the Internet are available 24/7. Maybe it is time for us to go back to the old song and ask ourselves the question, "What would we do if Jesus came to our house to spend a day or two?"

What would we do, but also, what would we say? Would we say some of the things we do if Jesus were standing right by our side? Would it not change things quite a bit if we only had a sense of His presence with us all the time?

As I have considered the church rumor mill issue, it seems to me that the root cause of the problem is the unconverted heart. We all know there is a spiritual war going on, and, as we discussed in the previous chapter, the battle rages between our two "natures."

Our spiritual nature understands that gossip is wrong, but our carnal nature fights for the supremacy. When we have been deeply hurt by others, it is a natural human reaction to lash back at them. If there are limited things we can do, there is always our tongue. How do we win this battle? The answer to that question is really the same as "how do I give my heart to Jesus, and be fully converted?" That is a question we need to consider every single morning as we start each day afresh and lay our sins at the foot of the cross. It is also the topic of the rest of this chapter.

God Understands

The good news is that even though God hates sin, He loves us so much that He made a sacrifice of His Son. While Jesus was on earth, He was tempted just as we are. Jesus understands our heartaches, our pain, our fears, and our propensity to sin. If we are truly sorry, willing to unconditionally surrender our sin, and ask Him to forgive our sins, He is willing to give each of us the victory over our earthly struggles. As our advocate, Jesus takes our sins to the Father. Jesus is like our attorney. He is on our side, pleading for our forgiveness, on our behalf.

"But why would God even forgive my sins?" Because so many people have been taught that God is harsh, unforgiving, and cruel, this is a question that has been asked throughout the centuries. The answer is found in one of the most profound scriptures in the entire Bible.

"For God so loved the world, that he gave His only begotten Son, that whosoever believeth in Him should not perish, but have everlasting life" (John 3:16). I get so excited when I read this verse because here we see the big picture of the universe. To me these are the most wonderful words in the entire Bible—and what an incredible difference in character between Christ and Satan. In contrast to Satan, a "thief" who "cometh not but for to steal, kill, and to destroy" (John 10:10), God "so loved the world."

But the plan of salvation instituted in heaven made a way of escape from mankind's transgression. God's plan of salvation covers every human ever born into this sinful world. John 3:16 tells us that "whosoever believeth in Him should *not* perish, but have everlasting life" (emphasis supplied). No one will be kept from entering heaven unless he or she chooses to miss heaven.

How do we obtain this eternal life? "If we confess our sins he is faithful and just to forgive us our sins, and to cleanse us from all unrighteousness" (1 John 1:9). "In this was manifested the love of God toward us, because that God sent his only begotten Son into the world, that we might live through him" (1 John 4:9). "Neither is there salvation in any other: for there is none other name under heaven given among men, whereby we must be saved" (Acts 4:12).

How beautiful are Jesus' words to us, for they are indeed the words of life. The only requirement for a sinner to be saved is to repent of his sin. When we confess our sins, He promises to answer our prayer.

"Behold, I stand at the door and knock," says Jesus, and "if any man hear my voice, and open the door, I will come in to him, and will sup with him, and he with me" (Revelation 3:20). This salvation is by grace, not works. And it is a free gift of God. "For by grace are ye saved through faith; and that not of yourselves: it is the gift of God" (Ephesians 2:8).

How to Miss Eternal Life

While some people want to know what they must do to be saved, others have wondered what they must do to be lost—not that they want to be lost—they just want to know what actions would result in the loss of eternal life with Jesus. The answer to this question is simple: the actions that will result in a sinner being lost are basically the opposite of those that result in salvation.

The Bible tells us that people who reject Jesus as Lord and Savior do not qualify for eternal life with Him. God, in His love for us, will not force anyone to spend eternity with Him if they choose to go elsewhere. Although the choice we make is often verbalized, our real decision is shown in our actions.

A person may profess to believe in Jesus Christ by his words while he disobeys God's law by his actions. The Holy Spirit speaks to each of us. Every time Satan tempts us to do something wrong, the Holy Spirit reminds us that we are God's, and we should follow God's law of love. If a person rejects the Holy Spirit's counsel to do what is right, then he or she sins.

The Definition of Sin

As Christians, it is of the utmost importance that we know and understand the Bible definition for sin. In 1 John 3:4, the Bible tells us that "sin is the transgression of the law," or the breaking of God's eternal laws of the universe. That's why it's so crucial for Christians to understand that God's eternal moral laws, known as the Ten Commandments, were not nailed to the cross. The laws against killing, stealing, and adultery (among other actions) are just as valid and binding today as they were back then.

Rebellion against God is called sin, and unconfessed sin ends in death (Romans 6:23). The Bible tells us that "all have sinned and come short of the glory of God" (Romans 3:23).

When a sinner chooses not to be sorry for His sins, Christ's blood cannot save them. "For the wages of sin is *death*, but the gift of God is *eternal life* through Jesus Christ our Lord" (Romans 6:23, emphasis supplied). So sin is the transgression of God's law, and when sins go unconfessed, the sinner inherits death instead of life. God does indeed love the sinner, but the sinner cannot inherit the kingdom of God unless he confesses His sins and asks God to forgive Him.

Easier to be Saved Than Lost

Despite the requirement that we must confess our sins, it does seem that it's easier to be saved than lost. Rightfully, we belong to God. Since the very beginning, we are His. God did more than create us: He created us in His own image. And though it's hard for humans to imagine, He loves us more than we love our own children. God is definitely on our side, and with His powerful help, it is definitely easier to be saved than to be lost.

Satan may be prince of this earth (John 12:31), but God is the King of the universe (Psalm 103:19), and the only creator God. The only way we can be separated from God for eternity is to reject Christ's shed blood on the cross of Calvary. We can make this choice by rejecting God's laws and living for self. This is exactly what Satan did in heaven. He chose to follow his own selfishness; therefore, rejecting God's perfect law of liberty, and, in the end, choosing death.

The whole universe is watching this great controversy between good and evil unfold. I believe the worlds that have not yielded to sin will ultimately see that when creation goes against the creator, that everlasting separation through death will come.

Satan didn't fall into sin; he chose to sin. Satan rebelled against God's eternal laws of heaven. When he rebelled, Satan chose not to spend eternity with God. And we too have a choice about where we will spend eternity.

While it's too late for Satan to repent, it's not too late for each of us to confess our sins and ask God to cleanse us from all unrighteousness (including the sin of a hurtful, unrighteous tongue). Won't you make that choice, and choose to lay your sins—whatever they are—at the foot of the cross today?

CHAPTER 8

The War Between Two "Commissions"

Have you ever worked with someone who had their own agenda or was trying to do just the opposite of what you were attempting to accomplish? Kind of difficult, isn't it? The prophet Amos had it right when he asked "can two walk together except they be agreed?" (Amos 3:3). The answer to that question, of course, is a resounding "No." When two parties work directly against each other, the work of one is going to be impeded. And that's exactly what's happening with the work of God and His church in this world.

Just before He left this work, Jesus gave His disciples the "great commission" to go into the entire world, teaching the gospel. We can read about this commission in Matthew 28:18-20, where Jesus says "All power is given me in heaven and in earth. Go ye therefore and teach all nations, baptizing them in the name of the Father and of the Son, and of the Holy Ghost: Teaching them to observe all things whatsoever I have commanded you: and, lo, I am with you always, even unto the end of the world."

Unfortunately for Christians, the devil has a "great commission" as well. He commissioned his demons to stop the gospel message from spreading. So there are two groups: one with a gospel commission and one with a diabolical commission, battling for the supremacy. The Bible warns us that we must "be sober, vigilant; because our adversary the devil, as a roaring lion, walketh about, seeking whom he may devour" (1 Peter 5:8). Satan will use any means of deceit to devour us. Faultfinding and gossip are two of the deadly tools in his arsenal.

The sad truth is, if you aren't actively working on Christ's side, you fall, by default, on the other. It's as simple as stop and go. If we are promoting the gospel of Christ we are doing what Jesus says to do. If, on the other hand we are trying to stop the gospel of Christ we are supporting the work of Satan.

Satan has made tremendous inroads in destroying the church of God on this earth by getting Christians so busy talking about each other that they "don't have time" to fulfill the gospel commission. Many Christians are so content with just "playing" church and warming the pews, they don't get involved in God's evangelistic army. When this happens, we become sitting ducks for Satan and his demons to deceive us.

My father often repeated the old saying, "An idle mind is the devil's workshop." I'm sure most of you have heard that statement also. Though it's not found verbatim in scripture, this principal is still very true today. If we professed Christians are not being used of God, we are "pawns" being used by Satan.

Losing Our "First Love"

Have you noticed that when a person first gets "saved," how busy they seem to be working for Jesus? It seems they tell everyone they meet about their life-changing experience. On the other hand, have you ever noticed that when professed Christians "settle in" and do no more than fill the pews at church each week, they become critical of everyone else? How easy it seems for Christians to join the church rumor mill.

I know I'm speaking quite frankly, but one of the main objectives of this little book is to awaken "Laodicean Christians." If we think we can fall asleep at the wheel and inherit eternal life, we are sadly mistaken. Going to heaven is much more involved than getting "saved" once. I know many of you will disagree with me, and that's okay. You may even feel you have read enough, slam this book shut, and move on to other things. That is also your right.

Nevertheless, it's important to understand that Christians gain much in terms of power when they work to fulfill the gospel commission. The very act of sharing our personal testimonies strengthens and refreshes us. When I witness to others about the victory I've found in Jesus, my testimony seems to rejuvenate even me. Has that happened in your life? The more I witness to others and see people accept Jesus

Christ as Lord and Savior of their lives, the closer I become to our precious Savior.

I have learned through the years that the greatest asset we have as Christians is our own testimony of what Christ has done in our lives. Why? The lost souls we are trying to reach do not really care how much we know about Jesus. They care about whom we know—not how much we know.

Some Christians will memorize whole books of the Bible, and that is a splendid achievement. But if I tell a drug addict about someone who memorized a whole book of the Bible, it won't help him break his addiction. Even memorizing the entire four gospels would not lead the lost to victory. Yet, the testimony of someone who has been freed from drug addiction can have a powerful influence on the life of another because a changed life, a life of religion "with boots on," is the most powerful witness. Hearing the gospel isn't always enough, but people really respond to a "sermon in shoes."

The Christian Version of "Show and Tell"

Most elementary schools have a program for the kids called "Show and Tell." The title of this "show" describes the duties of a Christian as well. We need to "show and tell" what Jesus has done for us.

Nothing hurts Christianity worse than when professed Christians don't live up to the gospel commission. Jesus spoke the words of this commission nearly 2,000 years ago; yet, the good news of salvation still hasn't reached the whole world. Technically speaking, it's possible to send the gospel over the airwaves at incredible speed. God's Word can travel to satellites placed 22,300 miles above the earth and return to the homes of billions of people at the speed of light—and that's 186,200 miles per second!

While Christian TV, radio, literature, and Internet networks send the gospel of Jesus into the homes of potentially hundreds of millions of listeners, and new souls are being reached for Christ every day, there are still places where the gospel isn't yet known.

A Lack of Commitment

"Why," you may ask, "with all the money and effort expended on missions, hasn't the gospel gone into all the world?"

The answer is that very few Christians in today's world take the gospel commission very seriously. Apparently they either don't understand their responsibility to get the gospel out to the world, or simply don't want to take part.

Another reason why the gospel of Jesus has not gone to the world yet is the fact that many Christians rely on their pastor, church, or some ministry to do what they should be doing. They financially support the idea of taking the gospel to the dying and lost, and even pray for the missionaries, but don't want to get "out in the trenches" themselves.

While Christians should support their churches and the ministries that God lays on their heart to bless with their resources, the fact that we give to God's cause in no way excuses us from personally witnessing to those around us. While there are myriads of excuses for not carrying out the great gospel commission, I don't see any of these excuses standing up in the judgment hall of the Lord Jesus Christ at His coming.

Lacking the "Gift of Gab"
Another frequently offered excuse for not spreading the gospel commission is that people claim that they "don't like to talk." "I just don't have the gift of gab," they say, or "I'm just too shy to talk to people."

I'm always amazed that, when these same people are hungry and visit a restaurant, they're never too "shy" to order exactly what they want. When people are negotiating to buy a home, car, or some other personal item, they seem to have enough of the gift of gab to get the job done. For some reason, however, many Christians become "tongue-tied" when it comes to their personal responsibility for taking the gospel "to the world."

People Make Choices
As Christians, we all make choices as to what is most important to us. If we have lost our vision to take Jesus to a lost-and-dying world, we will find excuses in abundance to support our decisions.

"People do what they want to do," my dad used to say. And the older I get, the more I see he was right. In most cases, people really do "do what they want to do."

If we are not personally involved in taking the gospel commission, we need to ask ourselves the question, "what is the priority in my life?" Is it to take personal responsibility for carrying the gospel of Jesus to the world? Or have I become so absorbed in the world around me that I've lost my love relationship with Jesus, thereby also losing my vision to witness to those around me?

These are questions I ask myself all the time because I believe that a lack of vision is one of the supreme reasons why the gospel of Jesus Christ has not gone to the whole world. "Where there is no vision, the people perish" (Proverbs 29:18).

If we want to stay focused on Jesus and fulfill His will for our lives, we need to have a clear understanding of what Jesus wants us to do while here on this earth. As His followers, God has entrusted us with a mission to accomplish before He returns.

If you haven't been a Christian all your life, you no doubt recall how excited you were when you first accepted Jesus as Lord and Savior of your life. No doubt you wanted to share your testimony with your unsaved friends and family, hoping that they would have the same experience you had. In your enthusiasm, you were probably willing to risk offending your friends and family in order to see them saved also.

Sadly, many Christians eventually lose their "first love." This may happen because the church they attend has lost its "vision for evangelizing." Sometimes Christians let their pastimes or businesses take priority over witnessing to the lost. Whatever the reason, we can be sure that Satan is behind it all.

Satan especially loves to work inside the church, because that's where he can "dilute" the gospel of Jesus the best. When men and women professing Christianity lose sight of Jesus and begin to "play" church, Satan can do the most damage.

An example would be the experience of "John Doe." Newly converted by the power of the Holy Spirit, John, as some would say, "got saved."

John found a church to attend, but soon figured out that something was wrong. The church members, and sometimes even the pastor, seemed more interested in keeping the church looking nice or even making sure it had money in the bank than they were in winning souls for Jesus.

At first, John attended all the business and board meetings he was allowed to attend. In vain, he tried to convince the "seasoned" members of his church that they should spend their time and finances in preaching the gospel to the world. He was very surprised at the opposition that quickly arose against doing what Jesus commanded the church to do.

As time passed, and John didn't succeed, he too became changed by the lack of enthusiasm for evangelism in his church. Slowly, and almost imperceptibly at first, he began to lose his first love, his zeal, and his excitement for soul winning.

Although the above experience isn't common to all Christians, most "seasoned" believers can definitely identify with the story.

We Do Not Have to Fail

The good news is we do not have to lose our first love or fail in broadcasting the gospel commission. In Matthew 28, Jesus tells us that "all power has been given to Him" (Matthew 28:18) to help us fulfill the commission. This is our assurance, or guarantee, if you will, that Jesus will supply everything we need to accomplish the task of disseminating the gospel to the world.

Years ago, I used to build houses for people. Most of my clients took a loan from the bank to finance their building projects. As a contractor, it gave me great confidence to know that the local bank had guaranteed all of the financial resources needed to complete whatever house I was building. Jesus' disciples had this kind of guarantee, or backing, as well. Before Jesus gave them the gospel commission to "go ye" into all the world, He guaranteed that He had the resources to carry them through. In fact, He signed the guarantee with His own blood on Calvary. That's why He could assuredly say, "All power is given me."

Essential for Our Salvation

When I really think about it, I realize that God could win the lost without my assistance. He could win the lost by Himself if He wanted because He is God. But that is not His plan. He has chosen us as the redeemed of the earth to show the world, by our actions as Christians, that through His shed blood on the cross of Calvary, we can be a victorious people. Christ did not shed His blood in vain. And He has commissioned me—and you—to go into the world to be a witness to others. Why did He do this? Because sharing Jesus in the marketplace is not just for the salvation of others, it's essential for my own salvation. Furthermore, our victory in Jesus vindicates God's name in the great controversy

Witnessing for Jesus by working to win lost souls helps take my focus away from "self." Satan loves to get people centered on self. He wants us all to have the "me, myself, and I" syndrome. This is indeed Satan's playground where he is the prince.

God knows human nature better than anyone, and He knows it is necessary for us to share our faith with others. That's why He gave the gospel commission.

"I just wish I could be a hermit," a man once commented to me. "I would just focus on my personal relationship with Christ and not have to worry about witnessing to others."

"I don't agree with that reasoning," I replied. "Working only for your own salvation is quite a self-centered thing to do." A true Christian disciple who loves his fellow man will most certainly want to share Jesus with those around him.

CHAPTER 9

Holding Your Peace

Before we get any further in this book, I need to make it clear that one of the reasons I know as much as I do about the "church rumor mill" is that I've had some experience with it. If you're honest with yourself, most of you will admit that you've also been part of the rumor mill at one time or another.

Like most people, I've been involved on both sides of the equation. Sometimes I've been the one who passed a rumor to others; at other times I was the subject of the rumor.

Nearly 25 years ago, the Lord impressed me to start a ministry that would reach the world. I had no money, no education in communications, and no property to start the business. I didn't really have anything that would make a significant contribution to such a worldwide ministry. I was so impressed by the Lord to go forward, however, that I did. This decision was, and still is, the best choice I ever made in my life.

Today, this ministry reaches millions of people with the gospel of Jesus Christ—around the world and around the clock. This success has happened through the power of God, who blesses us humans in spite of ourselves. God doesn't pour His evangelistic blessings on a particular person or ministry because the people involved deserve it. We are all sinful human beings in need of a Savior.

In starting this ministry, I was really just obeying the gospel commission to "go ye and teach all nations" (Matthew 28:18-20). This is a direct command which was given not only to the disciples of that day, but to all followers of Christ. The way I see things, if Jesus bothered to say it, then I should bother to listen and act on what He said.

Two Potential Responses

As a professed Christian, I can deal with a passage like Matthew 28 in one of two ways. I can try to exempt myself from the command with the excuse that it doesn't apply to me, or I can decide that if Jesus said it, I believe it. If I choose the latter, I need to take action. Even if I can't see what lies ahead, I must carry out Jesus' marching orders. If I go forward with the goal of taking the gospel to all nations without the physical means to do so, this is "stepping out in faith."

In my own personal relationship with Jesus, I have learned that faith doesn't even begin until my sight ends. If I can work out all the details in my mind and have all the resources to accomplish my mission, I'm not really stepping out in faith.

This type of faith isn't an "accepted option" in the business world. Before any business manager or CEO goes forward with a plan, he or she wants the project to look successful on paper first. That's not how Christ works, however. While planning is always a good thing, God wants us to step out in faith because He knows that such action will strengthen our faith.

The devil is a master at placing obstacles in the way of Christians to keep us from "moving forward" with our mission. It seems he has a million excuses ready, any of which we can use to "get off the hook." He also wants to discourage us from fulfilling God's plans by constantly reminding us of our failings and sinful nature.

None of those excuses are valid, however, because Jesus has promised us the necessary power to carry out His marching orders. "I can do all things through Christ which strengthens me," as He reminds us in Philippians 4:13. Also, in the fourth chapter of the same book, Jesus also reminds us that He will supply all our needs according to His riches in glory (Philippians 4:19). God is right there by our side, loving us, fighting our battles, and encouraging us to go forward and trust in Him. He will never leave us or forsake us.

The devil doesn't seem to bother me much when I'm doing little or nothing for the cause of Christ. As soon as I finally make a decision to trust God and go forward with His plan for my life, the devil finds a million ways to try to destroy me and the ministry I represent.

The Devil's Deadliest Tools

One of the devil's deadliest tools for destroying people or ministries is the "church rumor mill." Through it, he has destroyed the character and credibility of more than a few. Satan doesn't need the agnostics, atheists, and non-Christians of the world to help in this work. One of his greatest joys is using "Christians" to do his bidding.

Satan is a master of deception, a loser and liar who wants us to join in his deceit. When an agnostic attacks a Christian or his theology, church members easily see the threat and quickly band together to fight the enemy. But when someone carrying the name Christian attacks other Christians, the water gets muddy quite quickly. Suddenly those involved are divided. People begin to take sides in the war, and the rumor mill runs out of control as the "Battle of Tongues" erupts.

If we Christians want to win against Satan, we need to be much more prepared for his attacks than we are now. The Bible warns that a "*house divided* against itself shall not stand" (Matthew 12:25, emphasis supplied). Our house does not have to fall, however, and we do not have to be discouraged by the constant attacks from the enemy.

"Great peace have they which love thy law and *nothing* shall offend them" (Psalm 119:165, emphasis supplied). I have found that being offended is a choice. No one is responsible for my actions except me. When I'm attacked, I can choose to find peace in Jesus or I can become offended and defend myself. While it's a natural reaction to defend myself, the end result of that course has always been a disaster. I'm still learning to hold my peace and let God fight my battles for me.

I wish I could say that when we hold our peace, God will remove every storm, but that's not the case. He has promised to shelter us under His wings and bring us safely through those storms. And the trials and temptations we face are His tools for perfecting us, so that in the end we'll be like gold tried in the fire. Victory over the devil will be ours as long as we accept Christ and His righteousness into our lives. With God's help, we can defeat the devil whether he attacks us through the church rumor mill or any of his other weapons.

In the years since I made a big faith commitment to follow God's plan for my life, He's still providing my every need according to His riches in glory. Amazing as it may seem, I'm still on my feet going forward. And when the day comes that I do go to my rest, by the grace of God I plan to go there victoriously. Praise God. Satan will have lost another soul. And of course, this experience can be yours as well.

During my years of ministry I've seen hundreds, if not thousands, of times where the church rumor mill pumped out accusations against me and my fellow workers in the Lord's vineyard. This experience has led me to appreciate all the more the words in scripture that "all that will live godly in Christ Jesus shall suffer persecution" (2 Timothy 3:12).

It's not easy when we find ourselves amid controversy, especially when we're not guilty of the accusations against us. Being a fighter by nature, I want to defend myself. This is exactly what the devil wants any of us to do. He loves it when we operate on our own strength, because that's when he can really defeat us. When we put on the whole armor of God by submitting and committing our lives to Jesus, He will fight our battles for us. In the words of Exodus 14:14, "The Lord shall fight for you and you shall hold your peace." Isn't that great? God will fight for us when we hold our peace.

I don't know about you, but while I love the thought that God will fight for me, I sometimes think he still needs my help. Whoops. That's when I find myself in hot water. The key admonition in that scripture—that we should "hold" our peace—is sometimes much easier to talk about than it is to put into practice.

One of the toughest battles I've ever faced wasn't a battle against the secular world. It was a battle against the church rumor mill. A small group of people, including some ex-employees of the ministry where I've been involved, decided they didn't like the ministry leadership, which of course included me. They began to use the Internet to spread false rumors about the ministry and myself. The fact that these rumors weren't true didn't stop them from quickly making their way into churches across America, and as time went on, they grew by leaps and bounds.

The way these accusations about the alleged misuse of funds circulated and grew was nothing short of amazing. The church rumor mill really was running rampant, so rampant, in fact, that some of the worldwide leadership of the church to which I belong decided to distance themselves from the ministry where I was involved. This was quite a change, since they had been working with us for more than 20 years by that time.

One of the most serious allegations leveled by these individuals involved financial matters. Convinced that the ministry was misusing funds, this little group began sending a letter campaign to the IRS. Using fictitious names, they asked for a government investigation in hopes that enough violations would be found to charge either myself or the ministry with civil or criminal wrongdoing.

The articles that were printed and distributed discouraged people from supporting the work of the ministry. People I had never met used the Internet to tell stories about the alleged "misuse" of funds, among other allegations.

While I knew these rumors weren't true, and the ministry made every effort to convince supporters that there was no financial wrong-doing, many assumed that both myself and the Board of Directors were guilty.

Things became even more "interesting," if that's what you want to call it, one day when a couple of IRS investigators appeared at my door. Their agenda was simple: to discuss some information that had been sent their way. This was the start of an IRS investigation that lasted nearly a year. The IRS requested documents from the ministry's accounting department, outside auditors, and even the publishers of my books. Before they were done, they had requested and received more than 100,000 pages of documents to research. Understanding that these agents were simply doing their job and apparently wanting to do it thoroughly, we of course complied with every request they made. How relieved we were at the end of the investigation when the IRS closed the case without finding one single violation. No criminal or civil charges were made, and neither were we fined.

All of the accusers were proven to have given faulty information. Though they didn't have all the pieces of the puzzle, these accusers had felt they had enough information to decide that we had done wrong. Though in the end they were the ones who were proven to be wrong, a tremendous amount of damage was done. The IRS destroyed the more than 100,000 pages of documents covering six years of financial records, but the rumors still hung around. Once the rumor is out there, it can never be taken back.

Isn't that just like Satan? As the "accuser of the brethren," he rejoices every time a Christian falls into the trap of spreading rumors against other children of God (Revelation 12:10).

How About You?

You may be going through all sorts of pain and heartache today. Perhaps some of that pain is self-inflicted, but perhaps some of it is manufactured by the church rumor mill. Either way, Jesus is there to give you peace in the midst of the storm. All you have to do is ask Him to take over your life, and He'll do it today.

CHAPTER 10

Run—Don't Walk—
Toward the Trumpet

I n order to prepare for eternity with Jesus, I believe that we must each stay focused on God's plan for our lives and not allow ourselves to take a detour by Satan along the way. How do we do this?

We can start by having a clear understanding of what it is Jesus wants us to do while we are here on this earth. God entrusted His followers with a mission to accomplish before He returns to this earth in what is termed as Jesus' second coming.

We have already considered Matthew 28:19, 20, where Jesus admonishes us to "Go ye therefore and teach all nations, baptizing them in the name of the Father and of the Son, and of the Holy Ghost: Teaching them to observe all things whatsoever I have commanded you: and, lo, I am with you always, even unto the end of the world." Jesus is coming again, and our job is to help others be ready for that coming.

When Jesus came to earth the first time, He came as a babe wrapped in swaddling clothes, lying in a manger. When He returns as Lord of Lords, however, His appearance will make world news.

"Every eye shall see Him ..." (Revelation 1:7). Although His return to this earth will be short-lived, He will liberate His people from death, hell, and the grave. The Bible explains His second coming to earth like this:

> Behold, I shew you a mystery; We shall not all sleep, but
> we shall all be changed, In a moment, in the twinkling

of an eye, at the last trump: for the trumpet shall sound, and the dead shall be raised incorruptible, and we shall be changed. For this corruptible must put on incorruption, and this mortal must put on immortality.

So when this corruptible shall have put on incorruption, and this mortal shall have put on immortality, then shall be brought to pass the saying that is written, Death is swallowed up in victory.

O death, where is thy sting? O grave, where is thy victory? The sting of death is sin; and the strength of sin is the law. But thanks be to God, which giveth us the victory through our Lord Jesus Christ.

Therefore, my beloved brethren, be ye steadfast, unmovable, always abounding in the work of the Lord, forasmuch as ye know that your labour is not in vain in the Lord. (1 Corinthians 15:51-58)

Did you notice—the last verse in this passage expands on the great commission? In addition to helping get others ready for Jesus to come, Jesus is telling us to "be unmovable, unshaken, always abounding in work realizing that our work is not in vain." Praise God from whom all blessings flow.

A Key Ingredient of "Focus"

Truth is a key ingredient to keeping Christians focused on the mission to "go ye." Unfortunately, it seems that very few Christians today are willing to speak or stand firm for truth. Truth is just not very popular, even among Christians.

This is a travesty, for Jesus is all about truth. In the words of Jesus, we can know "I am the way, the truth, and the life" (John 14:1).

It is always my prayer that God will lead me into truth. I've been a Christian long enough to know that none of us have "all" truth. Left to our own nature, we will be deceived by Satan. "The heart is deceitful above all things, and desperately wicked" (Jeremiah 17:9).

To me, this verse simply means that I can't rely on my feelings since they are so frequently carnal. Every thought, feeling, and impulse

55

I have must be held up to the light of God's law. "To the law and to the testimony, if they speak not according to this Word, there is no light in them" (Isaiah 8:20).

As the "father of lies," Satan understands just how important truth is. That's why he's worked so hard to introduce watered-down versions of the truth into the Christian church. Tradition, which takes the place of solid doctrine built on the Word of God, seems to have crept into nearly every denomination. The sad result is that many churches—and individual Christians as well—have lost their vision or focus for carrying this gospel to the whole world. Many churches have become no more than a social club that is more focused on serving donuts and coffee instead of the pure Word of God. Such churches may provide a meeting place, and even do many good things, but the essence of the gospel is lost.

The most beautiful sound is the sound of truth ringing from the lives of professed Christians. Truth ringing from the lips is nice, and even important, but truth that rings and resounds from the life is the most effective of all.

When a Christian lives his life according to Bible principles, truth takes on a certain ring or sound that will indeed draw those around to the Jesus he serves. "For if the trumpet give an uncertain sound, who shall prepare himself to the battle?" (1 Corinthians 14:8).

Modern-day Gideons

The story of Gideon, as told in the Judges 6, provides an excellent example of what happens when the trumpet does "give a certain sound." I've always loved the story of God—and only 300 men—defeating a vast army that was more than 100,000 strong. No doubt the 300 represent God's church today. We are so few in number compared to the rest of the world; yet, with God's help, we must take this gospel of the kingdom into the whole world.

Have you ever noticed in the story of Gideon how the enemy actually destroyed themselves, right after Gideon and his men broke their pitchers and gave their trumpets a "certain sound"? It's a frightening thought, but if the church of today rejects the sound of the "trumpet of truth," it could be the army that's destroying itself. Without truth, the darkness is as black as night. There is noise and confusion all around.

The trumpet is heard in the distance, giving the "certain sound." But down in the camp, locked in their spiritual blindness, a vast army of souls seems bent on destroying itself. "Where there is no vision, the people perish" (Proverbs 29:18).

In the story of Gideon, the enemy was so confused and confounded that they turned on each other. They were also not prepared for battle and in a very sleepy state. Had they been alert, awake, and able to see, they could have easily defeated Gideon and his men.

Is there an important lesson we can draw from this story? Could it be that today, we as Christians are our own worst enemy? If we do not wake up, we could destroy ourselves.

Still, there is abundant hope for Christians, for the devil has no power over us unless we neglect a love for the truth.

Taking Our Eyes off Jesus

It is when we take our eyes off Jesus and choose loyalty to people, rather than the task of sharing the gospel, that we are divided. In the administration of churches and ministries, Christians are sometimes guilty of choosing friendships rather than truth.

We will plan, plot, politick, connive, and become divisive. And when we do this, we become a tool in the hand of the devil to destroy rather than grounding ourselves and others in the faith of Jesus, all the while telling ourselves that what we are doing is right. Convincing ourselves that our "mission" is to expose the sins of others to the world, we neglect to fall on our faces and in humility confess our own sins to our loving heavenly Father.

If we wish to stop the carnage and get back to our real mission, we must get back to God's truth. Understanding and holding firm to God's Word is essential to being and staying a Christian. It's one thing to become a Christian, but it's another thing to keep grounded and rooted in God's Word over the long haul.

Many people become involved in the emotion of a good, old-fashioned altar call. They genuinely do want Jesus as Lord of their lives. But while they take their stand to accept Jesus and become a Christian, within a short time they return to their previous lifestyles. The reason for this backsliding, most of the time, is that the individual has not become rooted and grounded in Bible doctrine. New Christians need to immerse themselves in God's Word. They need to do more than join a Bible-believing church. Attending a mid-week Bible study group is an excellent idea as well.

If we want to stay focused on the Christian mission, we need to know what we believe and not be blown around by every wind of doctrine. Doctrines, which are really the pillars of our faith, should never be eroded by time or circumstance.

The Ten Commandments are a prime example of a Bible doctrine that Satan wants to destroy. Through a misunderstanding of Scripture and diluting God's commandments, Satan works to get Christians to believe the commandments were nailed to the cross. We need to realize, however, that the fact that Jesus died for our sins doesn't give us a license TO SIN.

If we want to uncover these deceptions and "settle into the truth" so that we aren't buffeted about by Satan, there is only one way to do it: through continually and prayerfully studying the Word of God. In the process of becoming rooted and grounded in Christ, we can also greatly improve our walk by sharing what we have learned— both about the love of God and the beauty of Christian doctrine— with others.

In my own life, I have found that the more I share my testimony of what Jesus has done for me in saving my soul, the more my personal relationship with God is strengthened. By witnessing to others about Jesus, I am also confirming Him as Lord and Savior of my life. My love for Him grows even more as I share with others what Jesus has done for me.

God Doesn't "Need" Me

When I really think about it, God could win lost people without my assistance. In spite of this fact, He commissioned me to "go" into the world and witness to others. Why? Because sharing Jesus in the market place is essential for my own salvation, not just the salvation of others.

Satan loves to get people to focus on self. Witnessing for Jesus naturally takes the focus away from self. Even a newly converted or "baby" Christian can share his or her experience of becoming a Christian with others, and this is a great faith builder. When we share our personal testimony of what Jesus had done for us, it strengthens our faith by constantly reminding us that Jesus really does love us, and how deep that love really is.

If you have lost your focus on the gospel commission and are somehow wandering around in the darkness of the camp, why not abandon that noisy, confusing, and losing army? Run—don't walk— toward the light of truth and the certain sound of the trumpet. Grab your family and friends, and, as you run, get out your own trusty trumpet. God wants you in His army today.

CHAPTER 11

The Four "L"s Behind the Distractions

With his thousands of years of experience, the devil is a master at trying to get Christians to lose their focus. As Christians, we're supposed to be looking at the "big picture" in the war between Christ and Satan. We're also supposed to be growing more and more like Jesus by dying to self each day. Unfortunately, Satan knows how to "lull" us to sleep along the way. By throwing up smokescreens, he tries to keep us from focusing on our road map to heaven, God's Word. His goal is to get every Christian to lose sight of truth, and he has several favorite tactics for accomplishing this goal, which I have divided into the four "L"s of:

A. Legalism

B. Liberalism

C. Lazy-ism

D. Loose Tongue-ism

We fall prey to these four "L"s when we neglect the Word of God and forget to feed ourselves the spiritual food that will make us grow in the Lord. Although I have given "loose tongue-ism" an "L" all its own, each of these "L"s is closely related to faultfinding and gossip. In the next four sections, I'll provide some important information on how to be on guard for—and overcome—these deadly four "L"s which have wreaked so much havoc in God's church today.

A. The "L" of Legalism

Have you ever wondered why or how the Jewish leaders didn't even have the spiritual awareness to realize that Jesus was the Son of God? Were they intentionally a mean and uncaring people?

I don't believe they were, but I do believe they were deceived by Satan. God loves everyone, and yes, He loved those Jewish leaders who rejected the Son of God even though they had become so legalistic in their religion that they lost their spiritual eye glasses. The promised Messiah was finally here on earth to save His people, but they didn't recognize who he really was. Instead of welcoming Him as King of Kings and Lord of Lords, they crucified the Son of God.

This was supposed to be God's church, yet they chose Barabbas, a common thief, over Jesus. You can read the story in Matthew 17. Then, in addition to crucifying Jesus, they also killed most of His disciples.

"How could this happen?" "Wasn't the Jewish nation looking forward to the coming of the promised Messiah?" Yes, they were looking for the coming Messiah to save their people. This quite naturally does raise another question: Why then did the Jews not recognize the Messiah when He finally came?

Busy with Man-made Laws

A study of scripture shows us that the Jewish nation was so busy passing man-made laws that they forgot about the law of God. In place of a personal relationship with the Heavenly Father, they substituted religion. Sadly, the church of Christ's day understood very little about the very important themes of love, mercy, and compassion.

The church leaders of Christ's day also saw Him as competition to their leadership roles. In their human pride, they saw Jesus as a threat to their "church."

"Who does He think He is?" they mumbled to themselves. "He hasn't even gone to the 'theological seminary' for his religious education. How dare He show so much love and compassion to the common people?"

By ignoring their burdensome rituals and rules, Jesus offended the scribes and Pharisees. It seemed He threw all their man-made rules out the window. He even had the nerve to heal people from their sickness and diseases on the Sabbath day.

I'm sure many of these religious leaders honestly thought that Jesus was of the devil. They had never found the loving character of Jesus in their studies. As legalists they bound themselves and others to man-made rules. Others rejected Jesus because his perfect character of love was a constant reminder of their sinful nature. Some might have felt they'd gone too far in their legalistic, sinful ways to humble themselves before God and the people.

Jesus sought to correct these errors in the beautiful story of Nicodemus. Nicodemus was the leader who came to Jesus at night, asking how he might be saved. That's when Jesus told him that he must be "born again."

> There was a man of the Pharisees, named Nicodemus, a ruler of the Jews: The same came to Jesus by night, and said unto him, Rabbi, we know that thou art a teacher come from God: for no man can do these miracles that thou doest, except God be with him. Jesus answered and said unto him, Verily, verily, I say unto thee, except a man be born again, he cannot see the kingdom of God. Nicodemus saith unto him, How can a man be born when he is old? can he enter the second time into his mother's womb, and be born? Jesus answered, Verily, verily, I say unto thee, Except a man be born of water and of the Spirit, he cannot enter into the kingdom of God. That which is born of the flesh is flesh; and that which is born of the Spirit is spirit. Marvel not that I said unto thee, Ye must be born again. (John 3:1-7)

Trying to Keep God's Law

When I was a young boy, I had some of the same misunderstandings about the plan of salvation that Nicodemus did. I didn't really understand that it was a free gift from God. I knew I should keep the Ten Commandments, or "ten promises," as I call them now. But they just seemed like rules to be kept. I didn't understand I should keep them because of my love for Jesus. Without even knowing it, I had become a "legalist," or someone who tries to keep the law of God, but for the wrong reasons and without the power of the Holy Spirit.

I wanted to keep God's law in my youth, but it was a constant struggle. I thought I had to please God, so I could go to heaven. As a child, I had been taught that if I failed to keep God's law, I would go to hell and be "lost" forever.

My physical growth came naturally as time passed, but the spiritual growth wasn't so "natural." In my boyhood, I always wanted to go to heaven. As a young married man, I also wanted to go to heaven. However, I only kept the commandments of God because I wanted to be saved, not because I loved Him.

As a young person, I would have loved to spend Sabbath afternoons in front of the TV or on the ball field although my parents trained me not to do these things. Instead, they taught me to honor God on His Sabbath.

As I grew, my spiritual nature didn't mature nearly as quickly as my physical nature. While my physical nature cried out for attention, my spiritual nature seemed to be slipping away. My physical nature was crying out for more attention, so it was fed more than my spiritual nature.

My physical appetite increased with age as my body cried out for the attention it needed to grow and remain healthy. At the same time, my appetite for spiritual food such as God's Word diminished bit by bit. I realize now that this was because I was paying attention to my physical needs much more than my spiritual needs.

Even as a young married adult, I would much rather have been playing a ballgame than going to church or worshipping God on His Sabbath. I never really considered playing ball on the Sabbath, but it sure sounded like fun to me.

My desire to go to heaven rather than hell was still the driving force behind keeping God's Ten Commandments. This is what I had been taught as a child, and in my mind it stood to reason that I should obey all Ten Commandments—including the fourth.

Now that I have developed a personal relationship with Jesus, I look at the Ten Commandments so much differently than I ever have before. Now I see them, as one preacher stated, as the ten promises.

God promises that if I surrender my life to Him that He will give me victory over the physical temptations to kill, steal, commit adultery, bear false witness, covet, etc. Isn't that incredible?

I used to think the Ten Commandments were something I had to do to keep me from going to hell. But now I see them as a love letter from God telling me He will be there for me, and that He will give me victory over sin even when I stumble and fall.

Even if I do fail, if I am truly sorry about it, God lovingly forgives me and gives me a new slate to "write on." Christ's shed blood on Calvary did something for us that the Ten Commandments could never do.

We are not saved by keeping the law of God. We are saved by grace. Does that give me a license to sin? Absolutely not! "Do we then make void the law through faith? God forbid: yea, we establish the law" (Romans 3:31). The New Testament book of James confirms Paul's statement: "For whosoever shall keep the whole law, and yet offend in one point, he is guilty of all" (James 2:10).

The Bible calls God's law the PERFECT law of liberty, or the perfect law of freedom. It also tells us that those who keep God's law will be blessed in their deeds. Christ's death on the cross did not give us license to sin. Our freedom as Christians is not in breaking God's Ten Commandments, but in keeping God's Ten Commandment law. "But whoso looketh into the perfect law of liberty, and continueth therein, he being not a forgetful hearer, but a doer of the work, this man shall be blessed in his deed" (James 1:25).

Before I really fell in love with Jesus, I thought God would honor my actions if I didn't play ball on the Sabbath and went to church instead. What I didn't realize, at the time, was that God really wanted my heart—not just my outward actions. It wasn't until years later that I finally understood the difference between simply being "religious" and having a true, personal relationship with God.

I still struggle with the flesh, of course. And if you are honest, I think you'll admit you do, too. The difference is that I now serve God out of love. My relationship with Him has matured into a loving one, between my Heavenly Father and me.

"How long have you been a Christian?" is a question I enjoy asking many people as I travel around the world. I'm always amazed at how many Christians will answer by stating "I grew up in the church," or "I've been a Christian all my life."

It seems that somehow many people believe that growing up in the church makes them a Christian. This isn't necessarily the case, of course. In the words of an old saying, "You can put a cow in the garage for as long as you want, but it still won't make him a car." In the same vein of thought, growing up around Christianity does not make a person a Christian.

Sometimes people answer my question about whether they are a Christian or not by stating that they are "very religious." When this happens, I usually remind them that a person who drinks alcohol usually drinks "religiously." People who are hooked on drugs take them "religiously" and people who smoke cigarettes usually smoke them "religiously," too. Similarly, just because someone goes to church every time the doors open doesn't make them a Christian. It's possible to even dress, look, and act like a Christian without letting Christ into our hearts.

I didn't realize it when I was younger, but I fell into the "trap" of legalism. I wanted to be saved, so, as a legalist, I tried to live my life to the letter of the law whether my flesh wanted to or not. In other words, I tried to be saved by keeping the commandments of God. Although I would have denied it at the time, I was really trying to work my way into heaven. It didn't occur to me until later that keeping the commandments of God should be outward evidence that I have already been saved by the blood of the Lamb.

Today, I keep the commandments of God because I love Jesus. In doing so, I obey what Jesus told us to do: "If you love me, keep my commandments" (John 14:15).

Dangerous Folk Indeed

Unfortunately, legalists can be very dangerous to the cause of God. When Jesus walked the dusty roads of this planet, the Jewish leadership of His time wasn't just contemplating legalism. They were steeped in it. That's why they didn't recognize Jesus as the Messiah that they had been awaiting for hundreds of years. At the cross of Calvary, it was the legalists who shouted, "Crucify Him, crucify Him."

Many legalists are too busy finding fault with those who are focused on sharing the gospel to engage in sharing the gospel themselves. Most legalists I have known are not happy Christians. Worse yet, they often take it upon themselves to ensure that church members around them aren't happy either. Legalists have a low tolerance for anyone who doesn't agree with them. Living by the letter of the law themselves, they are first in line to disfellowship a brother or sister who may have made a public mistake. They are more worried about the embarrassment that might have been caused to the church, than loving and nurturing the wayward as the church family should.

Many years ago, I met an older couple who seemed very supportive of the ministry where God had placed me. They had a beautiful new home with more than 100 acres in Tennessee that they wanted to donate to my ministry.

There was one string attached, however. Someone had told them about seeing me eat fish at a restaurant one time. And it was true, I had eaten fish. For the most part, I am a vegetarian, but from time to time, I eat fish.

This dear couple was 100 percent vegetarian. And while they wanted to give so much to the Lord's work, they let me know that they wouldn't give the property unless I stopped eating fish. They didn't feel I could really be used of God if I ate fish.

"As much as we like your ministry," they told me, "we can't support you financially unless you make this commitment to us."

Since I wouldn't agree to abide by their health habits, they gave their entire estate to another ministry. The estate, which was worth several hundred thousand dollars, would have been a great blessing to our ministry. The truth is that it would have been worth never eating fish again for such a generous contribution.

I had noticed something about this old and very legalistic couple. They never seemed happy. Worse yet, no one around them seemed happy. These dear people were constantly finding fault with almost every one that came into their lives.

My decision not to yield to their demands wasn't based solely on not being willing to stop eating fish. I recognized a legalistic spirit about them—a spirit I didn't want to have to contend with in the years to come.

Sometime later, after the wife had died, I was asked to sing at her funeral. While at the funeral, a mutual friend shared what had happened during the last days of this woman's life. She had visited the now deceased woman, who had cancer, in the days just before her death.

"I am afraid to die," the elderly woman had told her. "I don't really know Jesus."

This was a truly shocking confession, for this woman and her husband had been Christians for more than 50 years. She had been a literature evangelist, worked in missions, and, together with her husband, given hundreds of thousands of dollars to the Lord's work. Yet, when it came time to die, she admitted she really didn't know Jesus.

Quite naturally, the dying woman's husband was very upset when she said she didn't know Jesus. But although he reminded her of all the years she had worked in ministry, she still insisted that she would be lost because she didn't know Jesus.

"I began to share the story of salvation with her," said the lady who told me this story. "I told her of Jesus' great love, and how He had showed that love through the plan of salvation." The Holy Spirit moved upon that sick woman, so that right then and there she accepted Jesus as Lord and Savior of her life.

The lady sharing this story then showed me a piece of paper written by the woman who had passed to her rest.

"Now I belong to Jesus and He belongs to me;" "I love Jesus, and He loves me;" "Jesus loves me;" and similar phrases were scrawled all over that paper. This dear elderly woman had been too weak to talk, but she could still scratch out notes to Jesus. That's what she did in the closing days of her life, and I was so blessed to be able to sing for her funeral. I still wonder at the marvelous grace of God, who understood the exact needs of this poor dying soul and never stopped reaching out to her until she finally understood that she was not saved by works alone, but by the grace of God.

I wish I could say the story of this once legalistic lady was an isolated one, but it is not. Warning signs surround the Christian church today; many of His followers understand very little about the loving character of the Jesus they claim to represent. This is especially true in their dealings with other church members. When it comes to showing love and compassion to the lost or even our Christian brothers and sisters, many of us are sadly lacking.

When Justice Meets Mercy

Legalists put a lot of emphasis on rules and regulations. And it's true; we need to value God's rules. God's Ten Commandment law is not just a set of rules given to the Jewish people, and it was not nailed to the cross. This is the eternal law of the universe—the same set of laws that will govern heaven for ages to come. What's more, God's Ten Commandment law is a transcript of His own perfect character.

Although the Ten Commandments were given to Moses at Mt. Sinai, they existed far before that time. If the law is really a transcript of God's character, then its precepts have existed for eternity, right along with God. When Satan coveted God's position in heaven, and swayed an untold number of heaven's angels to follow his lead, he and his followers were really breaking God's Ten Commandments.

"How could Satan have broken the Ten Commandments in heaven if they hadn't been given to Moses yet?" Frankly, there had to have been a law, or there couldn't have been a sin. The Bible tells us that sin is the transgression or breaking of God's law, and where there is no law, there is no sin.

While I learned about the Ten Commandments when I was a boy, and mentally understood that He wanted me to keep them, my main motive for keeping them was so I could get to heaven. Being young physically and young in the Lord, I had not developed a love relationship with Jesus just yet. That's why my service to him came from what I had been taught, rather than from personal experience.

"Experience is the best teacher," my dad used to say. And I have found this to be true, especially when it comes to growing my relationship with Jesus. It's possible to do many right things for all the wrong reasons, and that's what a legalist does. Jesus wants us to grow beyond that, however. Keeping His law is still important, but when we do what is right out of our great love for Him, that's when we're really growing in grace. It is possible, and even easy, for any Christian to fall into the trap of legalism. But my prayer for myself and others is that we will, by the grace of God; stay as far as we can from this snare of the devil.

B. The "L" of Liberalism

A "liberalist," in my opinion, has the same basic problem as the legalist: he or she doesn't really have a love relationship with God. Both the liberalist and legalist want to be saved rather than lost, but they go about it in different ways.

The legalist feels that by depriving himself of "things" he wants to do in the flesh, he will get God's attention and maybe even earn "extra credit." The "liberalist," on the other hand, often takes a liberal stand as a reaction to the legalistic influence of his parents, close family members, or other authority figures he or she knew as a child. Remembering all the "do's" and "don'ts," he or she determines not to follow in the footsteps of the legalists.

"These other folks in my religion are too legalistic," he or she says. "They live by too many do's and don'ts. I don't want my Christian walk to revolve around do's and don'ts, and I don't really think God cares so much about do's and don'ts, anyway."

"My Bible," the liberalist says, "states that we are saved by grace. Therefore, I am free from the law."

The liberalist doesn't recognize that faith and works walk hand in hand.

"All I have to do is confess Jesus with my mouth," the liberalist says. "I am not going to let my Christian walk get mired in works."

It is true that there is only one way to be saved from sin and death, and that is through the atoning sacrifice of Jesus Christ. In the words of the Bible, "Be it known unto you all, and to all the people of Israel, that by the name of Jesus Christ of Nazareth, whom ye crucified, whom God raised from the dead, even by Him doth this man stand here before you whole. This is the stone which was set at naught of you builders, which is become the head of the corner. Neither is there salvation in any other: for there is none other name under heaven given among men, whereby we must be saved" (Acts 4:10-12).

The Bible also tells us, however, that we must be doers of the Word, and not hearers only. In other words, if we are saved, the actions of our Christian life will confirm it.

In the words of the Apostle James, "What doth it profit my brethren, though a man say he hath faith, and hath not works, can faith save him? If a brother or sister be naked or destitute of daily food, and one of you say unto them, depart in peace, be ye warmed and filled, notwithstanding ye give them not those things which are needful for the body; what doth it profit? Even so, faith, if it hath not works, is dead, being alone. Yea, a man may say, Thou hast faith, and I have works: shew me thy faith without thy works, and I will show thee my faith by my works" (James 2:14-18).

Satan is so deceptive. He tempts the legalist to place too much emphasis on his works and the liberalist to place too much emphasis on his faith. As a friend of mine once said, "The devil doesn't care which side of the boat we fall out of, as long as we fall out."

Liberalists seem to think it's all right with God if we compromise our worship service to entertain church members, even if that means converting the sanctuary to look like it came right out of a Hollywood movie set. "Whatever it takes to get people to church" is what the liberalist thinks.

Liberalists can get especially riled up when other church members aren't willing to compromise on doctrines that have long been pillars of the church. Instead of staying within the principles or boundaries of Christian living, the liberalist wants to talk about the changing times in which we live and that it's really okay to compromise church standards.

The liberalist cares more about church growth than he does about the spiritual growth of the church. He feels that the compromising of "standards" is inevitable.

"If we want peace in the church, we shouldn't resist," he says. Liberalists are usually very vocal about their point of view. The fact they are usually a minority in many mainline protestant churches doesn't detour them a bit from infecting the conservative church with their theology.

Over the years, the liberalists have been quite successful in virtually every denomination. If you look at any mainline Christian church over the last 50 years, I doubt you will find any that hold to their original mission statement or doctrinal beliefs. Much of the responsibility for these negative changes lies directly at the feet of the liberalists. Sadly enough, the standards of dress and entertainment on many Christian college campuses is lower than on many secular campuses 50 years ago.

Each of us must examine our own hearts to ensure that we don't fall into the ditches Satan has so cleverly dug on both side of the road: legalism (on the "right"), and liberalism (on the "left").

C. The "L" of Lazy-ism

According to the last book of the Bible, the generation alive in the closing moments of this earth's history has a great propensity to be "lazy" Christians.

"Why is this?" For an answer to that question, let's turn in the Bible to Revelation 3:15-17:

> I know thy works, that thou art neither cold nor hot: I would thou wert cold or hot. So then because thou art lukewarm, and neither cold nor hot, I will spue thee out of my mouth. Because thou sayest, I am rich, and increased with goods, and have need of nothing; and knowest not that thou art wretched, and miserable, and poor, and blind, and naked.

What a rebuke God gives to this last-day church. While this verse makes it clear that our doom is not sealed, God points to our condition and asks us to repent. This rebuke is actually a good thing, for in the words of Revelation 3:19, "As many as I love, I rebuke and chasten, be zealous therefore, and repent."

The book of Revelation contains inspiration and hope for the "lazy" church of Laodicea. "Behold, I stand at the door, and knock: if any man hear my voice, and open the door, I will come in to him, and will sup with him, and he with me," and "To him that overcometh will I grant to sit with me in my throne, even as I also overcame, and am set down with my Father in His throne" (Revelation 3:20, 21).

What beautiful promises these are to those who keep their eyes on Jesus during these end times. We may have been born into the Laodicean church, but it's not God's will for us to stay in the Laodicean church.

"Well, how do I leave this sleeping church?" "How can I be part of the active, victorious church?" The answer is quite simple. Revelation tells us that the lazy and sleepy Laodicean church thinks they are wealthy and have need of nothing, when really they are poor, blind, and naked. It's hard to help someone who thinks they need nothing, so we need to ask God to help us see ourselves as He sees us. When we see ourselves as poor, blind, and naked—and not until—will we also see that we need a Savior to deliver us from the curse of sin. Satan loves to deceive us into thinking we are self-sufficient and self-sustaining. If we cry out to God for help, however, He will hear our prayers. Then we can experience true repentance and salvation.

71

When Christians accept the fact that we can do nothing of ourselves, but can accomplish all things through Christ who strengthens us, we will experience a new, loving, and exciting relationship with the creator God who has planned for our salvation since before the foundation of the earth was laid. Knowing that God has had plans for us from the beginning, and that we should be overcomers by the blood of the lamb and the word of our testimony, should give us great confidence and assurance that we are never alone to fight our own battles. And that is a very good thing because we definitely need His help to fight the fourth "L"—the "L" of "loose tongue-ism."

D. The "L" of Loose Tongue-ism

The last "L" is one of Satan's greatest tools—the loose tongue. This tool is so powerful that I was tempted to name this chapter "From Gospel to Gossip." And it does seem that many Christians today are much better at gossip than they are at sharing the gospel with the rest of the world. In the words of an old saying, "Bad news can travel around the world before truth can put its boots on."

I don't know about you, but I've seen this in action myself. Satan must take great pride in deceiving professed Christians into believing that they are doing good, when in reality they are breaking God's commandments and have unwittingly joined the team of Satan.

Because I believe in using every means possible to disseminate the gospel of Christ, I also believe that Internet chat rooms could actually be used for good. As I mentioned earlier, many "chat rooms" have become nothing more than "gossip rooms," places where professed Christians hide behind false identities and spend hours each day gossiping, slandering, and accusing other Christians. And this is all done in the name of Christianity. I really believe that the Christian church of today has more to fear from within that it does from without.

"Why do you say that?" I can almost hear the question being asked. Because Satan is the master of division, he could not survive in a church that wasn't divided. And while he will use any means possible to divide God's people, I believe he especially uses the media (including print, TV, and the Internet) to mesmerize Christians' minds. As a result, many Christians have totally lost focus of the mission statement of the followers of Christ.

Our Christian Responsibility

As Christians, we have a moral responsibility not to let the seeds of gossip grow in our hearts and minds. When a talebearer comes our way, accusing another brother or sister of wrongdoing, it's up to us to remember the source of that spirit. The spirit of our loving God is not the spirit of gossip. It is our duty to deny Satan a stronghold in our lives, even at the risk of offending the accuser. No doubt the church rumor mill would sputter and die if only each Christian would let the rumors die with himself.

The "Jim Gilley" Rumor

It's amazing how quickly gossip can travel. I was reminded of this recently when I received a phone call from a very good friend.

"Have you heard the latest report about Jim Gilley?" he wanted to know.

What has happened to Jim Gilley? A sick feeling came over me at the very thought of harm to this Christian brother. About a year ago, the board of directors in my ministry had asked Pastor Jim Gilley to take over the presidency of that ministry—a position I had held for nearly a quarter of a century.

I fully supported this move, believing it was time to bring someone new into leadership who loved Jesus, had experience in administering a non-profit organization, and supported the work our organization was and is doing to proclaim the gospel to the world. From its inception, I dedicated my life to maneuvering the mission of this ministry according to the dictates of the Holy Spirit. I loved this ministry and wanted to continue promoting Jesus through it. But I also knew that I needed to turn over the administration to someone else.

After several months of praying for the right person to take the helm, the board of directors asked Pastor Jim Gilley. Jim and his wife Camille graciously accepted this call, which he took as one ordained by God.

Just prior to the aforementioned phone call, Jim and I had spent several days with a large group of Christian business people who also count it a joy to give their time, talent, and resources to the cause of spreading the gospel to the world. It was a great experience. Jim and Camille had exchanged good-byes with my wife Brandy and me as they planned to stay a few extra days at Tampa Bay before going home.

Franticly, my friend demanded, "Danny, what's the latest report on Jim? I just got two phone calls saying Jim had a heart attack and is in a Florida hospital." I had to admit that I hadn't heard the tragic news about my good friend and neighbor Jim Gilley.

"I've been traveling, so maybe I missed a call," I told the concerned colleague on the other end of the line. "I'll find out what's going on, and call you back right away."

One of the things this phone caller and I have in common is that we want to make sure we have our facts straight before rumors start flying from church to church and around the world.

I said a quick prayer and dialed Jim's cell phone number, hoping maybe Camille would answer, so I could get a report. The phone had only rung twice when a familiar voice answered, however, and it wasn't Camille.

"This is Jim; what can I do for you, buddy?" I was so surprised I could hardly talk.

"I'm feeling better already," I told him.

"Why is that?" Jim wanted to know.

I didn't answer Jim's question at first.

"Where are you?" I wanted to know.

"I'm still in Florida," Jim replied, reporting that he'd gotten some good sun that day.

"You mean you didn't have a heart attack, and you're not in the hospital?" I finally had to ask.

"No, buddy, I feel great." Jim laughed.

So Jim really did not have a heart attack, and he was not in the hospital. I can't explain the relief I felt at hearing that he was fine. After quickly thanking the Lord, I began to wonder how and where such a rumor got started.

Though I probably won't ever know the answer to that question, I do know that the rumor wasn't the least bit true. Some people did believe it, otherwise they wouldn't have been spreading it through the church rumor mill.

Once again, this highlights a problem that is very prevalent in the world today. Many church members seem to be better at spreading gossip and rumors than they are at spreading the good news of Jesus to a lost-and-dying world. It is my prayer that, after people read this book, they will pass it to everyone in their congregation. I believe it's time that the church of God on earth moves from disseminating gossip to disseminating the gospel. How about you? Are you willing to let it begin with you?

How to Stop Rumors

"Can that be quoted?" This was the question one preacher I heard recommended we ask when we hear someone spreading a rumor. "Would you be willing to put that in writing?" is another question that often makes the talebearer sit down and think.

When someone tells me something bad about another person, I like to ask where they got their information. If they aren't willing to share the source the rumor, I don't want to hear anymore.

"Do you know for a fact that this accusation is true?" is another favorite question I like to ask. "If so, where is the proof?"

If the person tells me they do have proof, my next step is to ask if they have gone to the individual who is the subject of the rumor and confronted him or her.

"I'll be willing to go with you and talk to this person," I offer. In doing this, I am only following the advice of Jesus:

> Moreover if thy brother shall trespass against thee, go and tell him his fault between thee and him alone: if he shall hear thee, thou hast gained thy brother. But if he will not hear thee, then take with thee one or two more, that in the mouth of two or three witnesses every word may be established. And if he shall neglect to hear them, tell it unto the church: but if he neglect to hear the church, let him be unto thee as an heathen man and a publican. (Matthew 18:15-17)

If the individual spreading a rumor isn't willing to follow Matthew 18, I want no part in the matter. To take a part in this gossip is the same as partnering in sin with the perpetrator. Let us not forget that the problems in heaven started not only with pride, but gossip.

In the end, we will become what we behold. If we don't want to get detoured by Satan, we must constantly study God's Word, keeping in an attitude of prayer and daily commitment to God. Our lives should be centered around Christ and His Word, and that relationship—rather than rumored whisperings—should be the most exciting element of our lives.

The early church succeeded because "they were all with one accord" (Acts 2:1).

Now let me ask you a question: Does this "all in one accord" church sound like the church of today? Revelation 3 tells us that Satan will have the church of the last days in quite a sleepy state. Our only hope is to repent and ask God to remove the blinders on our eyes so we can see our sinful flesh as it really is. Without Jesus to cover us, we stand naked before the throne of God.

Many people worry that the government will take over the church and control it, while others feel just the opposite—that churches will take over the government. But I believe that some church members are the greatest enemies of God's church today.

As we look into this further, let us read what Jesus said in the Bible about the church of Laodicea: "I know thy works, that thou art neither cold nor hot: I would thou wast cold or hot. So then because thou art lukewarm, and neither cold nor hot, I will spew thee out of my mouth. Because thou sayest, I am rich, and increased with goods, and have need of nothing; and knowest not that thou art wretched, and miserable, and poor, and blind, and naked." (Revelation 3:15-17).

The church of Laodicea is in stark contrast to the early church in the book of Acts: "And when the day of Pentecost was fully come, they were all with *one accord* in one place" (Acts 2:1, emphasis supplied). Reading on, we find that "all that believed were together, and had all things common: and sold their possessions and goods, and parted them to all men, as every man had need. And they, continuing daily with one accord in the temple, and breaking bread from house to house, did eat their meat with gladness and singleness of heart. Praising God, and having favor with all the people, And the Lord added to the church daily such as should be saved" (Acts 2:44-47).

Don't those few verses about the early Christian church make you want to be part of it? If there's any doubt in your mind, consider these additional verses: "And with *great power* gave the apostles witness of the resurrection of the Lord Jesus: and great grace was upon them all. Neither was there any among them that lacked: for as many as were possessors of the lands or houses sold them, and brought the prices of the things that were sold, and laid them down at the apostles' feet: and distribution was made unto every man according as he had need" (Acts 4:33-35, emphasis supplied).

The good news is that we don't have to remain in a state of Laodicean sleep. We don't have to fall into the ditch of legalism, tumble in the other direction of liberalism, or succumb to the temptation of "loose tongue-ism." We can have victory over each of the four deadly "L"s, in Jesus. If you're not sure how to do that, please turn the page ...

CHAPTER 12

Victory in Jesus

W hen we truly invite Jesus into our hearts, we will act and think differently than we ever have. That's what the term "born again" means. We're so completely changed, it's like a rebirth. Jesus described this process in his late-night talk with Nicodemus when He said, "Except a man be born again, he cannot see the kingdom of God" (John 3:3).

When Jesus becomes Lord of our lives, we will want to share Him with the world. Our actions will change. Instead of constantly dwelling on the physical nature, our focus will shift to the spiritual. In making this dramatic change, we will be following the admonition of Scripture to be "doers of the Word, and not hearers only ..." (James 1:22).

When Jesus said, "If you love me, keep my commandments" (John 14:15), He was talking to people who have accepted Him as Lord and Savior of their lives. Jesus meant that if we really do love Him, we should do more than just talk about it; we should prove it. He doesn't just want us to "talk the talk." He wants us to "walk the walk."

There's no more beautiful sound than the sound of truth ringing from the lives of professed Christians. What do I mean by that statement? That truth coming from the lips of a Christian is not nearly as effective as truth coming from the life he or she lives.

This world will never be perfect until Jesus returns and purifies it, but He does expect His church to show His character to a lost-and-dying world. He wants us to lift Jesus high. In the words of scripture, "I, if

I be lifted up from this earth, will draw all men unto me" (John 12:32). We do not have to live defeated lives. We can be regenerated by the Holy Spirit to live a happy, healthful life here on planet Earth. For those who overcome, there is the promise that "to him that overcometh will I grant to sit with me in my throne, even as I also overcame, and am set down with my Father in his throne" (Revelation 3:21).

Easy to "Talk the Talk"

Unfortunately, the modern Christian church of today seems quite a long way from where Jesus wants us to be when it comes to lifting Him up. While many of us lift Him up in our talk, we fail to lift Him up in our walk. It always does seem easier to "talk the talk" than to "walk the walk."

We have good news in that we can jar ourselves out of this half-hearted, Laodicean sleep. "Dying" to self is a good place to start.

"I die daily," wrote the apostle Paul, and this must be the experience for every one of us. We must die daily to sin as Paul did. When a person is dead, they don't respond to anything. That's the way we need to be when it comes to the self-centered world of sin.

We humans have allowed Satan to trick us into an unbalanced serving of self. Jesus, on the other hand, wants His eternal family to follow the example of love and righteous living He demonstrated while on this earth. In fact, it's mandatory for Christians to follow Jesus' pattern of loving one another. If we are going to heaven, and heaven is to eternally remain a place free of sin, we must shed our sinful nature of selfishness and pride.

We can't change our human nature on our own merits, of course. We can only be changed by admitting our guilt and sinfulness and asking God to forgive us. "If we confess our sins, He is faithful and just to forgive us our sins, and to cleanse us from all unrighteousness" (1 John 1:9).

While we humans can never attain perfection by ourselves on this earth, we should be growing more like Jesus every day as we walk this road of life. Daily prayer and Bible study will draw us closer to Him, and the closer to Him we become, the less we concentrate on the carnal or physical world where Satan wants us to live. We grow closer to Jesus through constant communion with Him on a daily, hourly, and even minute-by-minute basis. We must walk hand-in-hand with God, seeking His guidance in our lives. The more we study the Bible, and the more we communicate with our heavenly Father, the more we will be like him. This process of becoming holy, or more like Jesus, is called sanctification as discussed in chapter 6.

If we fail to keep a strong and healthy relationship with Jesus, Satan will take advantage of every chance he gets to *deceive* us. That's why it's so important for Christians to stay in close communication with our heavenly Father through prayer, Bible study, and witnessing on His behalf. If we don't, we become easy targets for Satan to *deceive* us.

Praise God that we do not have to be *deceived* by Satan. Deception is a choice. Jesus showed us an example of one who came and lived on this earth and overcame death, hell and the grave. Even today, He gives his followers the same power to overcome as he overcame—not in our own strength, but in the strength of our loving Jesus. As we submit and commit our lives to Him, He covers ours sins with His blood.

In the Garden of Eden, Eve was "beguiled" by the serpent. In contrast, Adam chose to sin against God. He was not deceived. He chose his wife over God; he also chose sin over God and His love. The punishment was the same for both: they were removed from the Garden of Eden and *would eventually die*. Ever since that day, and for the ensuing 6,000 years, Satan has tried to deceive the entire human race.

Though Satan's goal was to destroy the inhabitants of planet Earth, there have always been Christian groups who held fast to the teachings of God's Word. These groups taught others the truth about our creator God, righteousness by faith, keeping the Ten Commandments, Christ's death and atonement for our sins on the cross of Calvary, and the second coming of Jesus. They taught others that if we submit and commit our lives to Christ, we could share everlasting life with Him. They also taught that Satan is powerless here on earth unless we voluntarily allow him to use us as a vehicle to do his destructive work.

A Wonderful Assurance

One of the greatest assurances we can get from reading Scripture is found in Psalm 91, where the Bible tells us that when Jesus is Lord of our lives, Satan can have no claim over us. Our souls belong to the God who created us. God will protect us from Satan, the enemy, so that he can't steal us for his purpose of separating us from God for eternity. We can only be lost if we choose to give our lives to the devil.

Jesus gave us an example of how to resist Satan's temptations when He fasted for forty days and nights in the wilderness. After Jesus was weak because he hadn't had anything to eat or drink for so long, Satan felt he could "prey" on Jesus.

"If you're so hungry, why don't you turn these stones into bread?" Satan wanted to know.

"But he answered and said, It is written, Man shall not live by bread alone, but by every Word that proceedeth out of the mouth of God" (Matthew 4:4). Jesus answered Satan with scripture, and Satan was defeated.

Thankfully, you and I have that same ability to defeat the devil today. All we have to do is answer his temptations with scripture, just like Jesus did. That's why Satan doesn't want Christians to study the Bible. He doesn't want them to find out the truth—that he's a defeated foe.

"All Power is Given Me"

When Jesus said "all power is given me" (Matthew 28:18), He established the fact that when you and I accept Him as Lord and Savior of our lives, we take on His character of love. He will give us the power to overcome sin in our lives, just as He did. And He will give us whatever tools are necessary to fulfill His command to "go ye" into all the world.

While we can't do anything without Him, we can do everything with Him. "I can do all things through Christ which strengthens me" (Philippians 4:13). Isn't that amazing? God has promised to give us power to defeat the devil just as Jesus did when He was tempted in the wilderness by Satan.

Now it's true that no one is perfect. In fact, none of us is even good. Because we have fallen into sin, there is no good or merit in us of ourselves. We are all sinners saved by grace—there is nothing we can do to earn us a place in heaven.

Salvation is a free gift. We receive it when we:

- Accept Jesus Christ as Lord and Savior of our lives,

- Acknowledge to Him that we know we are sinners, and

- Confess our sins to God, who is faithful and will forgive us and cleanse us.

God also gave us access to His divine nature through the Holy Spirit, who leads us into all truth. If we have fallen into sin, the good news is, it is not too late to change. If we take the counsel of the Bible and apply it to our lives, God will restore His blessings to us.

"If my people, which are called by my name, shall humble themselves and pray, ... then will I hear from heaven, and heal their land" (2 Chronicles 7:14).

Our lives should be a walking picture of what it is like to enjoy a personal relationship with Christ, but being a Christian doesn't mean we won't have any more storms in our life. With Jesus in our lives, we can have peace in the midst of the storm as discussed in chapter 9.

"Great peace have they which love thy law, and nothing shall offend them," wrote the psalmist (Psalm 119:165). "My peace I give unto you," were the words of Jesus in John 14:27.

Having been in ministry for many years, I've seen the ups and downs of the Christian walk. Nevertheless, we have no reason to worry about the future. The same God who has sustained us thus far holds our future in His hands.

As Christians, our future is bright if we are willing to trust Jesus and walk in faith. This road is not always easy, but when we trust the Lord and go forward by faith, He does supply all our needs. If we have accepted Christ's righteousness, we don't have to worry about the future, because God's Word says the righteous will inherit the earth (Psalm 37:29).

Most people read the back of the book before they buy it. They want to get some idea of the story line. If the book is a story book, the back may read something like this: "John and Mary rode off into the sunset happily ever after."

Reading the back cover first can later lead to a few questions. Suppose you buy this book, and halfway through it, find John and Mary falling over a cliff. Hanging from a cracking limb that could break at just about any moment, they are in danger of falling to their deaths 2,000 feet below the precipice.

What happens to you, as the reader, when you encounter this part of the story? Do you now believe that John and Mary will certainly fall to their deaths? Do you get discouraged and lay the book down, never to read it again? Of course not! Because you have read the back of the book, you know how the story will end. The back of the book has told you that, at the end of the story, John and Mary rode off into the sunset and lived happily ever after. Instead of becoming discouraged and depressed over the dire predicament in which John and Mary find themselves, you continue to read with great anticipation. Because you have read the back of the book, you are confident there is a happy ending. You may even feel a rush of excitement as you wonder how the author can possibly rescue John and Mary from this seemingly life-threatening scene.

That's how it should be with Christians. Even when the going gets tough, we should never get discouraged or defeated while traveling life's pathway because we've read the back of The Book. The "back" of the Bible says we are overcomers. It says we win. "And they overcame him (Satan) by the blood of the lamb and because of the word of their testimony …" (Revelation 12:11).

On Satan's "Most Wanted" List

Those of us who are active Christians are also on Satan's most wanted list. He seeks to destroy our love for our heavenly Father, devour us like a hungry lion, and demolish our walk with God. If it were possible, they (Satan and his colleagues) would "deceive the very elect" (Matthew 24:24). Never forget—Satan hates anyone who is a true follower of Christ, and he will use every tactic possible to exterminate their characters.

It's true; some of us may have to be John the Baptists before Jesus comes back. Being a Christian in the closing moments of earth's history is not for "sissies." It may cost us everything. Are you willing to make that choice to follow God—no matter the price? John the Baptist literally lost his head for proclaiming that Jesus was Savior of the world.

Throughout history, literally multitudes of men and women have lost their lives for the cause of God. Many were burned at the stake, many were beheaded, and many were subjected to cruel torture before giving their lives for the Master. In His overall "big picture" of working out the best good, God sometimes allows bad things to happen—even to His people.

Jesus clearly warned His disciples that they would be treated as He was, and that the servant was "not greater than his Lord." In the words of one of my friends, "As sinners, we all deserve the treatment that Jesus received from His chosen people ... torture and death." This could be called the Jesus treatment. "All that will live godly in Christ Jesus shall suffer persecution" (2 Timothy 3:12).

No "L"s in Heaven

One thing we can be sure of: while there will be many wonderful things in heaven, the four "L"s will not be there. Legalism, liberalism, lazy-ism and loose tongue-ism will be gone, destroyed with all other sin.

We cannot take these "L"s to heaven because they will not be allowed to dwell with perfection ... Worse yet, they are a positive hindrance to the cause of God on this earth. Why not give them up once and for all, so that we can, like the early Christian church, all "be in one accord"? Then the Holy Spirit can sweep through God's elect with great power, greater than any power this world has yet seen. Then Christians, filled with the Holy Spirit and focused on the great commission, will carry the gospel to the farthest corners of the earth. With the four "L"s forever out of the way, and our work as Christians completed, Jesus will come back to claim His true followers for eternity.

In this book, we've received a glimpse of the big picture. All we have to do now is to stay focused on our mission of heralding the good news of the saving power of Jesus to a lost-and-dying world. The great controversy between good evil, Christ and Satan, is all about who has a right to us for eternity. Because He created us and shed His blood for us on Calvary, Christ claims us as His own. On the other hand, Satan claims that because of our unconfessed sin, we have rejected God's plan of salvation and have chosen not to go to heaven.

"If God takes a sinner to heaven," Satan argues, "He is violating everything He stands for as a God of perfection." This in fact would be true, if God had not unveiled and put in place a plan of salvation for us. Praise God, for there is a plan of salvation whereby we who were born sinners may confess our sins to God. Because of Jesus' shed blood on the cross of Calvary, we may have right to the tree in life in heaven, with God forever.

I'm so thankful that when Jesus comes back to purify this earth with fire and we followers of Christ take our rightful place in the new heavenly kingdom, we can be sure that sin will never rise up again. We will be overcomers, and sin will be gone forever. "He will make an utter end: Affliction shall not rise up the second time" (Nahum 1:9). What a beautiful promise, and what a great place heaven will be.

As the Bible says, "Eye hath not seen, nor ear heard, neither has entered into the heart of man, the things that God hath prepared for them that love Him" (1 Corinthians 2:9). Sometimes I like to contemplate the goodness of God and try to imagine what heaven will be like, though I realize it will be far better than my "wildest" dreams.

As Christians, we constantly battle between good and evil. Indeed, a great controversy wages over our souls between Christ and Satan. Who will win? The decision really is ours to make. Salvation is a free gift from God. We can choose eternal life or eternal death

It is my prayer that each of us will choose eternal life with Jesus. While I like to concentrate on eternal things, I must also realize the importance of preparing for eternity now. I ask Jesus to anoint my eyes with eye salve that I might see myself as I really am—a sinner in need of a Savior. Thanks be to God that I am a sinner saved by grace. What about you? Have you asked Jesus into your heart and your life today?

CHAPTER 13

Getting Out of the Stall
(Taking Your Ministry
to the Next Level)

Y ou've probably heard the old adage: "An idle mind is the devil's workshop." "Thinking outside the box," or "getting outside
of the box" are also examples of phrases that are commonly
heard today.

For purposes of this chapter, I've decided to make up a phrase of
my own: "getting out of the stall." This phrase has to do with a true
story that happened to me a few years ago.

One of my friends, who I'm going to call "John," has raised and
sold horses for as long as I can remember. For many years, John kept
an average of 50-60 horses at his ranch. Due to age and health concerns, he finally had to make a tough choice. He just couldn't care for
his horses the way he once had, so he needed to sell them all.

One day while John still had his horses, I took a friend to his ranch
to see them. As we walked down a hallway in one of the barns where
the horses were stalled, we noticed something strange. The entire back
wall of one of the horse stalls had been removed, leaving it completely
open to the 100 acres of pasture outside. Only a 2 x 4 nailed across the
back of the stall was keeping the beautiful palomino inside from gal-
loping into the pasture.

If you've ever owned horses, you know a twelve-foot 2 x 4 isn't going to keep a thousand-pound horse from escaping out of its stall.

"I'm really surprised that mare hasn't escaped, with only that little
2 x 4 holding her inside her stall," I commented to John's grandson,
who happened to be working at the stables that day.

"That 2 x 4 isn't there to hold her inside," the young man replied. "It's only there to keep other horses from coming into her stall."

Looking more closely, I was shocked to see that the floor of this mare's stall was in very bad shape. There wasn't a single level place for her to stand in the whole 12 x 12-foot area. Anywhere she stood she was at an angle, which wasn't good for her feet. The stall didn't look like it had been cleaned in years, with manure buildup two to three feet deep in some places.

"That horse is four years old," the grandson told me. "She hasn't left that stall since she was very young." He went on to explain that when the mare was first born, John wanted to make her a show horse. He put her in the stall to keep her from the other horses so they wouldn't hurt her. But because of his age and health concerns, this beautiful palomino never made it to the show ring. In fact, she never made it out of the stall.

Some of the stable hands had tried to get her out, but she wouldn't let anyone near her. No one could get a halter or lead rope on her, and the longer she went without handling, the more cantankerous she became.

For most of her life, the only attention she got was at feeding time. No one petted or brushed her, and no one could get her out of the stall. Day after day, for several years, she had stayed in her self-imposed prison.

Once, John's grandson had decided it really was time to get this horse into the pasture. He recruited two other men to help with the job, but no matter what they tried, the horse simply refused to budge. Every time they tried to coax her out of the stall, she turned and started to kick. The men became so frustrated that they cut the back wall out of the horse's stall. If she would only step out, they reasoned, she could enjoy all the grass and water she wanted. She would be free to roam as she pleased.

Though this idea sounded great to the men, the horse wasn't the least bit cooperative. She had no idea of the "heaven" waiting outside.

"Is it OK if I try to coax her out?" I asked the young stable worker. Knowing that I was a long-time friend of his grandfather, he reluctantly agreed.

Going around to the back of the barn, I removed the lone 2 x 4 that was tacked to the stall. Opening the stall door, I then waved my arms in hopes that the mare would bolt out. Still, she would have no part of it. When I tried to enter her stall, she backed up to me, ready to kick with full force. Since she outweighed me by about 800 pounds, I quickly decided to avoid a physical confrontation.

Walking down the hallway, I found a long 2 x 4. Sliding the stall doors back only 12 inches or so, I began to prod at her legs with the board. She didn't like that very well, so my strategy seemed to be working. She went to the opening and seemed about ready to jump. Each time, however, she turned around and faced me again. I continued prodding at her, all the while yelling at the top of my lungs in an effort to scare her out.

My friend and I continued this tactic for several minutes without giving the mare a rest. She continued to go to the opening, but she just couldn't make herself enter the big pasture land. We kept right on prodding, however, and after awhile, she finally had enough. Once again she acted like she would jump—and suddenly, to our surprise—she did.

After all those years cooped up in the stall, I expected the mare to celebrate her freedom by racing across the 100 acres of pasture. She didn't seem to realize that her world was bigger than 12 x 12 feet, and so she started to run in small circles.

Her circles did become larger and larger, though, as she continued running. It must have felt pretty good to her, for soon she was prancing around with her head held high. Suddenly the light went on in her brain. There was more grassland to roam out there. Snorting loudly, she raced excitedly into the pasture.

Later that night the sight of that beautiful palomino horse, first "trapped" by choice in a smelly stall, then racing deep into the pasture, kept coming into my mind. And the Lord reminded me how we, as His creation, sometimes act very much like she did.

That horse was in a rut. Day after day, she went through the same routine. Her whole world was a 12 x 12-foot stall. She could do nothing but go in circles. After a few years of going in circles and never leaving the stall, she became comfortable with her surroundings. So comfortable, in fact, that when the owners offered her freedom, she wouldn't take it.

In many ways, we humans are like that horse. Jesus wants to give us freedom from the rut or prison of sin that dominates our lives. Day after day and year after year, we become comfortable in our prison of sin. We get so comfortable that, even when we do hear the good news of salvation and the freedom we can have through Christ, we are tempted not to accept it. And sadly, many people today are never making it "out of the stall." Satan has so deceived God's creation on planet Earth that most can't even comprehend that heaven is waiting for them.

God's followers also get in a rut when it comes to the gospel commission. God has asked us to take the gospel to the whole world. He's also promised to supply all the tools necessary to accomplish this mission. Many times, however, we go in circles just like that horse, accomplishing virtually nothing. At some point we get comfortable in our rut, so much so that we no longer realize we have fallen far short of our mission given by Jesus.

But this world won't be lasting much longer. With all my heart, I believe that our time on this earth is short. Jesus is coming soon. This makes it all the more important for Christians to "get out of the stall." We need to escape the rut that Satan has trapped us in, to experience the joy of salvation in the same way that horse galloped around the pasture. Together, we must spread this gospel of Jesus Christ to the whole world.

I know many Christians who are still in the stall running circles, accomplishing very little for the cause of Christ. It doesn't have to be this way, however. All we have to do is to take that first step in faith. There is freedom out there—freedom to do what God calls us to do.

For years, the palomino mare in this story chose a 12x12-foot stall filled with muck and manure over a pasture land full of freedom. The memories of freedom she had known as a young filly were clouded by her surroundings to the point where that filthy stall was actually her choice of a home.

As Christians, many of us have become comfortable right where we are. We have allowed Satan to blind our eyes, which have become so clouded that we've lost our first love.

Do you remember the wonderful feeling you had when Jesus first came into your heart? Do you remember what it was like when He first became Lord of your life? That's what the first love is like. That flame of "first love" quickly flickers and dies, however, unless we stay close to Jesus. We only keep that first love if we spend time with God every day, studying His Word and praying for His direction.

Like the horse in the stall, we may be mired down by the muck all around us. When this happens, we are only going through the motions of being a Christian. We have forgotten the victory God can give when we seek Him first.

Everyone who becomes a Christian lays their bad habits and issues at the foot of the cross when they first come to Jesus. How sweet it is when that happens. I remember how excited I was to give a testimony whenever I could, telling how God supplied all my needs. Whether those needs were spiritual, physical, or financial, I always knew God was there.

Yet, as time goes on, it's easy to lose that first love. We may even lose our vision. The Bible gives us a warning about that: "Where there is no vision, the people perish" (Proverbs 29:18). How important it is that we keep our first love, so we don't fall into this trap. We must also die to our sins, by asking Jesus to be Lord of our lives every day.

Satan is a pro at causing us to lose sight of the fact that Jesus Christ is Lord and Savior of our lives. He wants us to be complacent, for he knows when we get that way, he can use us in spite of ourselves. Yes, amazing as it may seem, Satan can use even professed Christians to be mouthpieces for him—all in the name of the Lord.

Such Christians are unhappy with their surroundings and unhappy with things at their church. Dissatisfied, constantly complaining and finding fault with others, they are now in a position where Satan can use them in the "church rumor mill."

Our time is short here on planet Earth, but with God's help, we can keep our relationship with Jesus fresh and new every day.

"And ye shall seek me, and find me, when ye shall search for me with all your heart" (Jeremiah 29:13). What a beautiful promise this is. It doesn't matter about our past. God forgives our sins and casts them to the depths of the ocean (Micah 7:19). Whether we are complacent Christians who have lost our vision, or the vilest of sinners, God will be there for us.

Most people I know are looking for peace of mind, but they're not going to find it in their little "stall." Only a love relationship with Jesus can give us that peace. Let's be like the horse that finally came out of her stall. Why not experience all that God has for us to enjoy here on earth?

"Great peace have they which love thy law, and nothing shall offend them" wrote the Psalmist (Psalm 119:165). Wow. What a beautiful promise. Even if the church rumor mill is chewing you up and spitting you out, as the old saying goes, you can still have great peace in your life when you love God and keep His commandments.

CHAPTER 14

The Deadly Tongue

The Bible refers to the tongue as deadly in the book of James:

My brethren, be not many masters, knowing that we shall receive the greater condemnation. For in many things we offend all. If any man offend not in word, the same is a perfect man, and able also to bridle the whole body. Behold, we put bits in the horses' mouths, that they may obey us; and we turn about their whole body. Behold also the ships, which though they be so great, and are driven of fierce winds, yet are they turned about with a very small helm, whithersoever the governor listeth. Even so the tongue is a little member, and boasteth great things, behold, how great a matter a little fire kindleth! And the tongue is a fire, a world of iniquity: so is the tongue among our members, that it defileth the whole body, and setteth on fire the course of nature; and it is set on fire of hell. For every kind of beasts, and of birds and of serpents, and of things in the sea, is tamed, and hath been tamed of mankind: But the tongue can no man tame; it is an unruly evil, full of deadly poison. Therewith bless we God, even the Father; and therewith curse we men, which are made after the similitude of God. Out of the same mouth proceeded blessing and cursing. My brethren, these things ought not so be" (James 3:1-10).

In addition, the Bible tells us that no man can control his tongue although it does not say that God cannot control our tongues for us. It merely says we humans cannot control our tongues. The Bible is also clear that we can do all things through Christ.

The devil rarely tempts human beings on their strong points. That's why many Christians are not tempted to physically kill a human being, for instance, but Satan often tempts us in spiritual killings or character assassinations, which has already been addressed in chapter 4.

Satan does not tempt me with alcohol, for example, because I've never consumed alcohol in my life. He does not tempt me to smoke cigarettes or do unlawful drugs because I've never had a history of doing those either. But he does tempt me, indeed, with my tongue, and I'm sorry to say that I have failed many times. That's when I go to Jesus and tell Him I'm sorry and ask Him to forgive me.

The Bible also tells us in Proverbs 18:21: "Death and life are in the power of the tongue." This is why it is so important that we asked Jesus to guard our tongues and not fall into the trap of joining the church rumor mill.

I'm inclined to believe that more Christians will lose eternal life with Jesus because of their tongues than the breaking of all the other commandments combined. The tongue is such a small thing but since it controls the rest of the body it makes sense that it is the very first thing Satan attempts to control. If he controls our tongue, he controls the rest of us.

I believe if we asked most Christians if they use their tongue for lying on a regular basis, the answer to the question would be "no." I am amazed that many Christians believe that one can lie in degrees; therefore, they make some lies worse than others. Have you ever heard someone say that they only told "a little white lie"? The only lie in that situation was the lie that Satan fed them that there are degrees to lying. "A lie is a lie, is a lie," as the old saying goes.

Have you ever asked yourself what a lie is? I have. The picture that I get from looking at a lie from a biblical perspective is that a lie is a distortion or compromise of the truth for whatever reason that it was spoken. That is why I earlier made the statement that I believe that the Christians greatest fear should be the fear of compromising truth.

There is no such thing as a little white lie, a partial lie or even a half truth. Any percentage of truth that is compromised now makes it a lie. Confusion through deceit has got to be one of Satan's greatest tools.

Most Christians that I know would not tell an "out-and-out, bold-faced" lie. But they will hand down one rumor after another about fellow brothers and sisters in Christ to other itching ears. Again, there is no difference or degrees when it comes to lying. The Bible says that Satan is the father of lies. So if I allow him to use my tongue to continually lie, then I must be a son of the father of lies. I know this sounds very intense, but I guess it is meant to get your attention. Knowing and recognizing this truth can mean the difference between life and death to you and me.

We need to realize that when we are part of the rumor mill, truth will be distorted or compromised. Some of my fondest memories of childhood were when our church family came together for fellowship. We would often spend time together, usually on a Saturday night to play games together. One of the games I remember playing as a group was for everyone to sit around in a circle. The host would whisper something in a person's ear. The goal was for everyone to whisper this statement to the ear of the person sitting next to him. The last person to receive the statement would audibly tell everyone what was passed on to him. Then the host person would tell everyone what was originally said. Guess what? The end result was always totally different than what was originally passed around.

It is no different today when it comes to the church rumor mill. The end story is totally void of truth. This, of course, makes us a party to a lie.

The Bible has strong counsel for those that take part in lies. In addition to the following verse, we can find many other texts admonishing us not to lie.

> He that overcometh shall inherit all things: and I will be his God, and he shall be my son. But the fearful, and unbelieving, and the abominable, and murderers, and whoremongers, and sorcerers, and idolaters, and *all liars*, shall have their part in the lake which burneth with fire and brimstone: which is the second death. (Revelation 21:7, 8, emphasis supplied)

94

In speaking to the scribes and Pharisees, Jesus said, "Ye are of your father the devil, and the lusts of your father ye will do. He was a murderer from the beginning and abode not in the truth, because there is no truth in him. When he speaketh a lie, he speaketh of his own: for he is a liar and the father of it" (John 8:44).

When we judge someone falsely, we have lied. I have no doubt that when Jesus described Satan as a murderer, He also meant "spiritual murder"—in other words, assassinating one's character. In the sight of God, physical or character assassination murderers will not enter the kingdom of heaven. Folks, it is imperative that we understand this point.

As I mentioned, Satan usually doesn't tempt us on our strong points. He knows that he can't successfully tempt most Christians to physically kill someone. Christians are too much aware of "Thou shalt not kill." So his great success within the Christian church is to trick people so that they become part of the church rumor mill where character assassination occurs everyday.

When we falsely accuse someone of wrong doing we are playing into Satan's hands. As tough as it may sound, we become little Satans. The Bible says that Satan is the accuser of the brethren (Revelation 12:10). If we constantly point our finger at others and accuse them of wrongdoing, we also fit the description of the scribes and Pharisees who Jesus said were sons of their "father the devil."

James wrote, "For whosoever shall keep the *whole law*, and offend in one point, he is guilty of all. For he that said, do not commit adultery, said also, do not kill. Now if thou commit no adultery yet if thou kill, thou art become a transgressor of the law" (James 2:10, 11, emphasis supplied).

Plainly speaking James tells us that we are accountable to keep ALL of God's commandments. Some people seem to think that keeping the commandments is like going to a smorgasbord for food—we can pick and choose which commandments we want to keep. This again is a lie from the father of lies, the devil. Breaking the ninth commandment of "Thou shalt not bear false witness" is no different than breaking the seventh commandment of "Thou shalt not commit adultery."

With all of this said, we should not be discouraged if we have fallen into Satan's trap, whatever trap that may be because the Bible tells us in 1 John 4:16 that "God is love." Moreover, John 3:16 tells us that from the beginning God knew we would need a Savior to redeem us from that hands of Satan. Knowing that, He sent His Son Jesus to die on Calvary's tree for your sins and mine. Because of His sacrifice, no sin is so great that God can't forgive it. Isn't that great news?

If you would like to ask Jesus into your heart today I would like you to repeat this simple sinner's prayer with me:

Dear Jesus,

I know that I am a sinner, and I am truly sorry for my sins. I realize that I cannot save myself. So, I am asking you to forgive me from all my sins and to cleanse me from all unrighteousness. Thank you Jesus for hearing and answering my prayer; in Jesus name, I pray … Amen.

When you pray this prayer you are not alone. Praise God for 1 John 1:9 that says, "If we confess our sins, He is faithful and just to forgive us our sins, and to cleanse us from all unrighteousness." Isn't that so incredible that God could love us sinners so much that He willingly pardons, totally and completely, all of the bad things we have ever done in this life?

My reason for writing this little book is not to criticize sinners as we all are sinners, but I was impressed to bring to light a subject that seems to have received very little press in recent years. My hope and prayer is that each of us draws closer than ever to Jesus and looks forward to His soon appearing, at which time we can look up into the clouds and say, "Lo, this is our God and He has come to save us."

Just because we ask Jesus to forgive us from our sins, doesn't mean that Satan will leave us alone. I believe that Satan's attacks will substantially increase. But I am thankful that we have a God who promises to provide every need. He may not deliver us from the storm, but He will surely deliver us through the storm. Therefore, let's commit to God to put on the whole armor of God every day so that we can withstand the attacks of the devil. Let us remember that God is love, and as His people, we should rightly reflect His character within our lives so that Jesus will shine on a lost-and-dying world, for the Bible says, "And I, if I be lifted up from the earth, will draw all men unto me" (John 12:32).